Insights

Talking Stick 29

Insights
Talking Stick 29

A publication of the
Jackpine Writers' Bloc, Inc.

© Copyright 2020 Jackpine Writers' Bloc, Inc.
Menahga, Minnesota
Printed in the United States of America
All rights reserved by the authors.
ISBN #978-1-928690-45-0

www.thetalkingstick.com
www.jackpinewriters.com
Send correspondence to sharrick1@wcta.net or
Jackpine Writers' Bloc, Inc., 13320 149th Avenue,
Menahga, Minnesota 56464.

Managing Editors: Sharon Harris, Tarah L. Wolff
Copy Editors: Sharon Harris, Marilyn Wolff, Niomi Rohn Phillips, Tarah L. Wolff
Layout, Production, and Cover Design: Tarah L. Wolff
Editorial Board: Marlys Guimaraes, Sharon Harris, Mike Lein, Ryan Neely,
        Tarah L. Wolff
Judges: Poetry Judge Sharon Chmielarz, Creative Nonfiction and Humor Judge
        Jill Johnson, and Fiction Judge Candace Simar
Cover Artwork: watercolor painting *Missing You* by Joanne Cress

Contents

Co-Editor's Note

Sharon Harris

Editor's Choice: "Shattered" p.104, Sue Bruns

My editor's choice this year is "Shattered" by Sue Bruns, page 104. I love this poem. I've done this, dropped a dish and watched it head for the floor, imagining that somehow it might stay whole. I've watched it explode into pieces and shoot in all directions across the room. The description of how these broken bits show up again and again is exactly what happens, days and weeks later.

Then the poet compared this shattering to a broken relationship. I've done this too, watched what I thought was a lovely connection start to slip, then end in chaos. I've watched and felt the shards of memories coming back, over and over, hurting me again, when I thought I was all over it.

Shattered too is the nice, neat, easy world we used to have. It sure seems that way now, looking back. While we all struggle with the strangeness of "our new normal," we all feel broken and on edge and off kilter.

We are all missing parts of our lives, parts of ourselves, scattered and away from many loved ones, trying hard to keep our lives intact, trying to find the glue that will hold us all together till this is over.

And, in many ways, we are all grieving for the loss of the life we knew—grieving for the changes we didn't expect and didn't ask for, grieving for the distances we have to keep. I hate to think that we might be all wearing masks and gloves for the foreseeable future, unable to see each other's smiles!

Hopefully we will all come out of this stronger, braver, more patient, and knowing ourselves better than we do now—with more insights.

Co-Editor's Note

Tarah L. Wolff

Editor's Choice: "Plainsong" p.133 , Norita Dittberner-Jax

Every year my mom and I have a tradition of going to the green house in the early spring and choosing far more annuals than we usually have places to plant them. She passed her love of flowers and plants on to me.

After an endless winter there is almost no better balm than stepping into the hot, growing air of a green house in late May. Considering this was May 2020, it might have never felt so good as it did this year.

Normalcy. A tradition filled with blooms and dirt. The same as it is every year even though we (and the world) were not. Norita's poem "Plainsong" (that I chose for my editor's choice this year) reminded me of this. How important some traditions can be to ground us, to remind us that life goes on living.

Over the years the plants and blooms have taught me something extraordinary. Plants choose us. Peonies chose me. I can transplant, neglect, put them anywhere any time of year and, somehow, they will always do fine. Tulips die beneath my hand even before I buy them. (I swear if I even look at them in the store they will wither at my glance.)

My mom, on the other hand, is loved by bleeding hearts. (I couldn't keep a bleeding heart alive to save my life.) This May, hers were up and blooming gloriously at no extra effort of her own beyond what she does for all of her perennials and annuals.

Same as me. We do it because we love to plant, not because we know they will do well . . . though we do hope.

In this year of nothing normal, it's good to realize that there are many things totally unaffected—such as bleeding hearts and peonies and moms and daughters in the sunshine, surrounded by flowers.

Poetry

First Place "Parting Song," p.1. Laura L. Hansen is the author of *The Night Journey; Stories and Poems* (River Place Press, 2020), *Déjà Vu* (Finishing Line Press), and *Midnight River* (NFSPS Press) which was a Midwest Book Award Finalist and winner of the Stevens Poetry Manuscript Competition. She lives on the Mississippi River in Little Falls, Minnesota.

Second Place "The New Dog," p.8 Marsh Muirhead

Honorable Mention
"The Echo of Her Shout," p.21 LeRoy N. Sorenson
"Quercus," p.68 J. M. S. Swanson
"Lake House," p.19 James Bettendorf
"We Stripped Off Our Wet Clothes," p.30 Joel Van Valin
"She Gracefully Stepped Aside," p.33 Dawn Loeffler
"After Office Hours," p.164 Nicole Borg
"Shattered," p.104 Sue Bruns

Poetry Judge Sharon Chmielarz's latest, twelfth, book of poetry is *The J Horoscope*, 2019. Previous books have been finalists for the Independent Book Publishers Award, Midwest Book Awards, National Poetry Series, and the Next Generation Indie Book Awards. *Kirkus Review* named her *The Widow's House* and *The J Horoscope* one of the 100 Best Indie Books of 2016 and 2019. You can visit her at www.sharonchmielarz.com.

Creative Nonfiction

First Place "The Cut Glass Bowl," p.2. Marlene Mattila Stoehr lives in Shoreview, Minnesota. She earned her Bachelor of Science degree from the University of Minnesota and a Masters in Intercultural Communication from Vermont College of Norwich University. After retiring, she served as an editor for an evaluation-consulting firm.

Second Place "Flying Minnie," p.9 Sue Bruns

Honorable Mention
"Mother's Mojo," p.47 Bernadette Hondl Thomasy
"Josephine Holding Deloris," p.87 Audrey Kletscher Helbling
"A Prairie Girl Sees the Ocean," p.107 Cheyenne Marco

Humor

First Place "The Plumber," p.7 Pam Whitfield (Poetry). Pam is an English professor, journalist, poet, and horsewoman in Rochester, Minnesota. She's performed spoken word, acted in plays, and she has done street theatre at the Renaissance Festival. In 2010, Pam won the MnSCU Educator of the Year award. The Carnegie Foundation named her Minnesota Professor of the Year in 2011.

Honorable Mention
"The Legend of Doug Dagnus," p.97 Paisley Kauffmann (Cr. Nonfiction)
"The Ladies Who Brunch," p. 135 Dorothy Anderson (Cr. Nonfiction)
"Dumboy," p. 153 Maurice Spangler (Fiction)

Creative Nonfiction and Humor Judge Jill Johnson wrote *Little Minnesota: 100 Towns Around 100* and *Little Minnesota in World War II: The Stories of 140 Fallen Heroes from Minnesota's Smallest Towns*. She is the series editor for the Little States series with Adventure/Keen Publications. Her latest book, *A Tale of Two Basketball Towns and Their Coach Jim Musburger* won recognition from Sports Authority as one of the top 18 basketball books in 2020. Jill and her husband Deane are the founders of Beagle Books in Park Rapids.

Fiction

First Place "The Last Day," p.4 Kathryn Knudson.

Writing has been a big part of Kathryn Knudson's life since she was young. She attended the Perpich Center for Arts Education, focusing on creative writing, and has continued to write and publish in the decades since. Kat lives in Minneapolis with her husband and their sheep dog.

Second Place "The Eighth Step is Amends," p.11 Paisley Kauffmann

Honorable Mention

"The Mangler," p.79 Kim M. Bowen
"Blind Date at Penny's Diner," p.161 Jennifer Hernandez
"Cora Comes to an Understanding," p.53 Victoria Lynn Smith
"The Astrophysicist's Wife," p.115 H. A. Brown

Fiction Judge Candace Simar lives in Pequot Lakes and began her writing career after attending a Jackpine Writers' Bloc workshop in 1999. Her work has since received awards from the Western Writers of America, Women Writing the West, The Will Rogers Medallion, the Laura Awards for Short Fiction, *The Writer's Digest,* The Midwest Book Awards, Brainerd Writer's Alliance, The League of MN Poets, The Lake Region Writers and other regional awards. Learn more about her work at www.candacesimar.com.

In memory of
Luke Anderson
1937-2020

I am a poet
in search of words,
measures, and
metaphors,
to resolve the enigma
of my time being.

from "Time Being"
by Luke Anderson

Insights

Talking Stick 29

Laura L. Hansen

First Place Poetry

Parting Song for the
Vanilla Strawberry Hydrangea

I
have taken
to touching
the springy heads
of the hydrangea
as I pass on my way to
the mailbox or on my way
to the street to walk the dog.
They are at their peak and I am as
proud of them as a parent sending their child
off to college. The blush of hope and sudden change
is on their cheeks. I cup them in my palm, the bright white
clusters still soft and moist, flexible in my hand, tender.
The ones that have matured to deep pink, to maroon, to
dusky brown show their age, bristle against my skin, like children
who know they are too old now for the public humiliation of hugging.
You know how kids of that age can be. They are ready to own the world,
to move on and yet, for now, they allow these secretive touches,
these last tender moments, their many-hued heads bob in the breeze
as if inviting my adoration, playful and ready to please. They are,
in this moment, my everything, loved by bees, dressed in butterfly wings,
touched by late August sun, and by my arthritic hands that understand
how the change of season pulls the moisture from the skin, saps
energy away from the limbs. I feel it as I pass their joyful gathering,
the winter that is sure to come, how their buoyant
cone-shaped

heads

will soon

be reduced

to tinder for the fire.

Marlene Mattila Stoehr
First Place Creative Nonfiction

The Cut Glass Bowl

Dishes are stored in the kitchen cupboard of my childhood memories—the oversized black pan full of three-day rolls of family fame, the crazed white platter, the enamel pot where my mother brewed tea leaves at the back of the wood stove. Nearby, the sides of white dishpans are splotched with blackness where the enamel is chipped; the grey coffee pot stands ready to boil coffee for District 51 PTA meetings, Christmas programs and picnics.

Our kitchen, as others of that era, had no wall-mounted cupboards. A freestanding cabinet doled out dinnerware—plates often mismatched, cup handles occasionally missing, chips never taken seriously. A pullout work shelf over the silverware and utensil drawers divided the lower storage compartment from the two main sections of the top. Behind the left door was a flour bin with a built-in sifter; behind the right our entire stock of plates, cups, saucers, and glassware. Important letters, none more important than those from sons serving in the Pacific, a Marine and two sailors, were filed next to the plates, signaling assurance of the boys' safety a short time before. The top center space held larger dishes and smaller bric-a-brac. Here my mother kept the cut glass bowl.

Intricately cut with prisms and patterns, perhaps six or seven inches across, the bowl broadcast a ringing tone when snapped with a finger—the mark of fine glass, we were told. Our tiny house offered no place for it to be displayed and admired. Never was it used for a serving bowl; it was too special for that. It was the *cut glass bowl*. There was an aura to those words.

As long as I can remember it had been there in the cupboard, a wedding gift to my parents. That much my younger sister and I recall, but we never asked from whom the gift was received. Now the last of eight surviving children, we pool our memories and pose the question. But it is too late; neither of us has an answer.

Sometimes, as we washed and dried supper dishes by kerosene lamplight, a wood fire crackling in our cook stove, Mother told us about working in Duluth as a domestic when she was yet a young girl. She spoke of learning the "proper" way to run a home, the rules for keeping a kosher kitchen, the etiquette of serving guests in Duluth mansions.

Though these stories could have sounded like "Cinderella Visits the Palace," they did not. Through disappointments, difficulties, and extreme poverty of the Great Depression, my mother retained her self-esteem. She felt no less worthy for having such a humble home, and so, for the most part, neither did we. It might have been on such evenings that we took out the cut glass bowl to look at and admire, to snap it carefully and hear its clear ringing tone.

The Last Day

Jackie had no idea how a day she didn't want to end could drag on so long.

During normal shifts in the Pipin' Hot Pizza area she prepped for the evening rush, then got a jump on the next day. But today wasn't normal. Shortened checklist done, she leaned against the counter, unable to block out Barb and Maryann gossiping behind the registers. She really didn't care about the implement dealer's new hair plugs.

Her eyes rolled to the clock above the sink. Six hours and Qwik Stop Shoppe would be closed for good. Or bad.

She realized Barb was talking to her.

"What?"

"You coming to Cuddy's?" Barb repeated, more patiently than Jackie figured she deserved.

The bar offered half-price beers to people losing jobs. It was getting to be a tradition.

"Nah, I just wanna get home to the girls."

This was true. Partly. Jackie also didn't want to spend her night reminiscing and getting depressed over times she'd already felt depressed about the first time around.

The town's grocery store closed a couple years ago. Then the café. Now the gas station. When they heard The Cents Store was coming in, and across the street at that, they knew. Qwik Stop Shoppe made its money on products, not gas. Sure, this spot would remodel as a Casey's; they were "invited" to apply for their old jobs. And there was Subway and Pizza Ranch out by the freeway. But the town was losing itself.

Jackie's cell rang, an old-fashioned landline tone.

"Gotta take this," she mumbled, more to herself than the others.

As she hurried toward the storeroom, she heard Barb's attempt at a whisper. "Poor kid. Bet it's the clinic again. Her mother always smoked like a chimney around her."

She also thought she heard Maryann respond, "Poor kid? Poor all of us."

Jackie focused on the phone call.

By the time she emerged, the station was full of chattering teenagers freed from school. She wove through them, not meeting anyone's eyes. Back in the pizza area, she tried focusing on whether she had enough slices. Tried and failed.

A senior smiled politely before plucking cheese bread from the warmer. Jackie felt a hundred years old. Was it really only eight years since she'd been that girl? She wanted to blame Chad and his deep blue eyes, eyes both daughters inherited, but she knew it was as much her fault. Taking care of a baby, working, and driving over to the community college had been too much. She dropped classes. Next thing she knew she had two girls in less than three years. She could almost hear her mom sighing. "Like mother, like daughter."

Her mom. The cancer.

Her boss told her she was a hard worker. Jackie got her first raise the same week Chad got his second DWI. That was it. She and the girls moved into an apartment above the laundromat. Now both were in school and she was taking an online class. Their next-door neighbor babysat in exchange for food (Jackie got a discount) and cigarettes (she promised not to smoke near the girls; Jackie chose not to think about it).

A three-pizza order came in, followed immediately by a double. The rest of the shift was a blur. Suddenly, it seemed, the floors were mopped for the last time, lights clicked off.

"Maybe we'll all get hired back," Barb offered, as they stood by the front doors, "and can meet at Cuddy's to celebrate."

Jackie could tell not even Barb believed this.

She slipped into the sweatshirt she used as a coat, trying to think of something to say. Nothing seemed right.

Maryann pushed into the cold. Jackie followed. They heard Barb lock the doors. Neither glanced back.

In her warming car, Jackie finally let herself think about the call. A smile transformed her face. She knew they'd find out soon, but for now the secret was hers. Well, hers and her boss's. Only one reference and still the clinic hired her. Impressed by "the longevity at her current position," they offered her the top of the hourly rate. Jackie had nearly screamed into the phone. She didn't tell them she'd stayed partly out of fear no one else would give her a chance.

She'd get benefits. And retirement. She laughed. She would become someone who had investments. The medical system even had locations in Arizona and Florida. Arizona! Florida!

Jackie drove past the pumps, old life in the rear-view mirror.

Pam Whitfield

First Place Humor (Poetry)

The Plumber

I bet the girls fell all over you
when you were younger
your straight teeth
your wavy hair
those eyes that go almond-edged
with sympathy in each corner

I bet the girls rubbed their small hands
up and down the prairie
of your chest, the nipples
popping up like gophers,
saying: *I'm here!*

I bet they fell in love
with your vocabulary
your penchant for Keats and Rawlings
the motorcycle rides
how their pleasure came first

I bet you didn't realize
that when I saw you
in the waiting area
I turned to take my daughter's hand
to hide my shock at your size

Your pants couldn't keep up
with your haunches
as you rose from the too-small seat
flashing flab and skin seam

I could have laughed.
But I was sad,
thinking:
That ass used to turn heads.

Marsh Muirhead

Second Place Poetry

The New Dog

The old dog is teaching the new dog old tricks—
how to paw at the door to go in or out,
how to bite back when your playmate
puts his teeth too far into your leg or tail,
how a scent can lead to danger or adventure.

The old dog, my dog for eleven years,
looks to me for approval: "See how good
I can be to this interloper, the one who will
steal your love from me," she says, "when I
can no longer hold my pee, no longer fetch."

I scratch the old dog in the way we know—
under her ears, along her belly, hard on her hip.
I bury my nose into her fur, inhale what we are,
knowing what we know in our own ways of time
and affection while the puppy bites and chews
his way into the future the old dog can feel and see
in her aching bones, in the bottomless well of her eyes.

Sue Bruns

Second Place Creative Nonfiction

Flying Minnie

"It's a perfect day for kite flying," I say.

From her hospital bed, Jayne can see the trees beyond the courtyard, bending in the wind.

"I've never flown a kite," she says.

The next breezy day, I pick up a small pink kite at the Dollar Tree and bring it to the nursing home. Jayne is in her wheelchair—feeling better after the antibiotics started working on another urinary tract infection. She watches as I pull the plastic kite out of its sleeve, pop the stays into place, and attach the string.

"Minnie!" Jayne says. Minnie Mouse's head dominates the kite. Decked out in oversized shoes and pink polka-dotted dress with matching bow between her large black ears, she smiles, her flirtatious eyes rimmed in long black lashes.

"Let's give her a try," I say, and Jayne's smile is almost as broad as Minnie's.

I toss an afghan over Jayne's legs, place the kite on her lap, and wrestle the cumbersome wheelchair through the doorway toward the front exit.

Aggie witnesses our escape, wheeling herself down the hallway to follow us. "Where are you going?" she asks.

"Kite flying," says Jayne.

"I've never flown a kite," says Aggie.

I push Jayne's chair into the fresh autumn air and park it on a patch of lawn near the pavement. Then I go back for Aggie and push her wheelchair to where Jayne waits. This autumn day still holds some summer, and Jayne insists on facing the sun. The wind teases the treetops as the sun plays hide and seek in the clouds.

Aggie and Jayne are years apart but they've become good friends over the past several years. On the days when Jayne stays in bed, Aggie wheels herself down the hallway to Jayne's room. Aggie's hearing aids are useless props. Jayne's MS limits her ability to speak loudly enough for Aggie to hear, yet they communicate, often without words.

Today, side by side, they watch as the wind carries Minnie upward. The breeze tosses Jayne's red hair. Before long Minnie is dancing in the clouds, her smile, like Jayne's and Aggie's, never fading.

I hand the spool of string to Aggie.

"Hold on," I tell her. "Just let Minnie dance with the wind." Minnie sways gently back and forth as the wind obliges. Aggie smiles, clutching the spool.

"Isn't she beautiful!" Jayne says. I'm not sure if she means Minnie or Aggie. Either way, she's right. Time is frozen by the dancing pink kite. We are neither now nor then, well nor ill, old nor young.

"Now it's your turn, Jayne," Aggie says.

Jayne's MS has robbed her of most voluntary movement. One hand retains limited use. I place the spool in that hand and wrap her fingers around it. We gaze up at Minnie. She is one of us, free to move about in the wind but tethered, nonetheless. And we three, earthbound, are in the air with Minnie, cradled in the hands of the wind.

Paisley Kauffmann

Second Place Fiction

The Eighth Step is Amends

After the unexpected death of his father, Max wanders between grief and anxiety. The autopsy results had determined his father died of arrhythmogenic cardiomyopathy, a genetic condition increasing the risk of abnormal heart rhythms and sudden death. The cardiology clinic, unconcerned with the urgency of his hereditary and likely fatal situation, scheduled Max for their earliest appointment, eight weeks out.

His mother decides to sell the farmhouse. She solicits his help to declutter and clean before she contacts the Realtor. Max thinks of his bedroom with baseball-themed wallpaper and hockey trophies. It seems impossible that he was dreaming of varsity cheerleaders and flexing in front of the mirror only a decade ago.

After an early flight and a long drive, Max finds his mother dragging a cardboard box across the porch. Her blond hair is tied back with a red bandana. A black smudge on her forehead seems to mark her for loss. Squeezing his hand, she thanks him for coming and leads him into the barn.

"Most of these are rusted," she says, nudging a bucket of nails with her foot. "I figured you weren't interested in this old stuff."

Max nods and investigates a pile of refuse: tattered work gloves, a broken shovel, and a dented stainless-steel flask. He turns the engraved flask over in his hands.

"Oh, that," she says. "That was his reminder."

"Reminder of what?" Max opens the cap and sniffs. "I didn't think he drank."

"He quit drinking the day we met."

"Did he have a problem?" Max asks, replacing the cap.

She tosses him a fishing reel, frizzy with line. "Here, look at this."

"He bought this for me on our first hunting trip. I was ten."

"Do you want it?"

"I won't fish." Max shakes his head. "Not without him."

"There's more stuff in here than I realized." His mother wipes her brow, stretching the black smudge into a gray streak. "I'm going to start dinner."

Max opens another cabinet. Curious, he removes a metal box tucked in the corner. He fingers a pink barrette and baby spoon. A few pictures, diluted with time, mystify him. An unknown family with bright smiles is seated at a picnic table. In another, his mother, soft with youth and mischief, sits cross-legged on a beach surrounded by three children with a baby in her lap. The oldest boy, maybe seven, has brown hair and eyes, as does a girl of four or five. Another younger girl, with hazelnut locks, wraps her arms around his mother's neck. The baby, wide-eyed with a dollop of chocolate curls—the baby, he believes, is him.

Under the photographs, yellowed newspaper pages are folded with precision. Max unfolds the top page. Dated twenty-seven years ago, the article describes a tragic accident over the July holiday weekend. "A drunk driver hits a family of six in a head-on collision." The father and three children were killed, only the mother and infant survived. Max unfolds the second newspaper. A recap provides a mugshot of the alleged drunk driver, his father. With dark circles and greasy blond hair, his young father stares through him. Max drops the page and covers his mouth. His heart pounds, an urgent reminder of his terminal condition. Gripping the workbench, he concentrates to slow his breathing.

"Ready to eat?" his mother asks.

Max startles.

"Well, you look like you've seen a ghost," she says.

Max turns away from the workbench, revealing the open box.

Her face falters. "I wanted to tell you, but—"

"It can't be true."

"Please." She drops her chin. "Let me explain."

"I can't believe you never told me."

"There was never a good time. First, you were too young, just a baby, and as you grew, life moved forward so fast, it seemed unnecessary."

"He killed a family."

"He did." She pauses and searches his face. "But do you understand who they were?"

"What do you mean?" He examines the headline. "Were they famous or something?"

"No, not famous." In a small voice, she says, "It was our family. Your brother, your sisters, and your real father."

"What?" Max steps back. "What are you talking about?"

She presses her soft palms to his stubbled cheeks.

In the morning, Max wakes before the sun and starts coffee. He rinses his swollen eyes with cold water in the kitchen sink. The world seems uncertain and fragile, but in the silver light of the new day, he inhales, calls the cardiology clinic, and cancels his appointment.

LeRoy N. Sorenson

Poetry

The Language of Loss

On this prairie, the houses
of the dead are left empty.
Soot is all that remains. Soot
and this armchair in the corner,
one leg gone; some dishes
in the kitchen and one dented pan
sitting on a rusted iron stove.

Most of the house stripped bare,
floorboards warped. It's hard
to imagine any life here—especially
when the wind bays.
Soot falls three stories down
from the attic, graying the wainscoting,
graying the peeling wallpaper,

graying the air I breathe.
Steps unsettle the boards below
my feet. The attic littered
with broken tools, a rocking horse
lying on its side. Two
bibles thrown in a corner
and discarded winter coats still
hanging in a closet. I stand

in the middle of a slanted attic
floor. What can I offer
them in their death?
Prairie dust—something lighter than the soot
of their lives. Or quiet? Like the rustle
of elms in a mid-summer haunting.

Merlot

I loped you around the arena as he cleaned your stall.

We both loved him.

Every circle I shared my secrets and fed you helpings of hay.

I could learn farming and be his morning kiss and his midnight cuddle.

My body precisely the perfect shape to be held by his forearms like cylinders of comfort.

I told you that I understood how you look at him as your guiding purpose to provide your best performance every time he was riding you and how after you would shake your majestic mane and nuzzle him like a telling of trust.

That same day when all his chores were done and our little talk was over, I led you to him. Every time your hooves met the dirt you snorted like together we won something and our victory was knowing we both believed in our bond.

When he showed me how to put my first foot in your stirrup and then to just toss my other leg over you, I knew like him I was someone special.

He told me to raise my right arm and suddenly we were circling like we were going to disappear into another world and then my left arm and before I could harness the moment or feel the wildness that suddenly consumed me like a spell, my smiling face found his face and his eyes were the color of distance. Where was he that day standing there giving me directions?

He named you Merlot after your coloring and of course the wine that when consumed makes bodily contact more seductively enchanting. I should've known like any other lesson that you can't come between a man and his horse.

Micki Blenkush

Poetry

By the Light of the Christmas Tree

Dancing with my daughter on a Saturday evening
LED overlapping circles cast
against the floor and ceiling like a disco
she's far too young to have known.
We take turns choosing songs—
"Stayin' Alive's" pointing and grooving.
"Back in Black," "Uptown Funk,"
our cat skittering in panic.
We've drawn what curtains we have
and try to avoid the bare windows.
She's less than a month from thirteen
and I turned fifty last summer.
We alternate inventing moves—
the goat, the geyser, the hummingbird
for which we flutter fast our hands
pretending to sip from red bulbs.
This artificial tree perfect to prance around,
each ornament hung with the same stories
she's heard year after year.
Rudolph she wanted to watch
twenty times a month and dinosaur facts
she used to spout. Glitter and Popsicle sticks
frame long-ago faces. How she looked
when we used to dance year-round.
Always an event, costumes and stuffed animals
arranged in advance. For once I don't ask
if she remembers. We laugh at one another's steps
as we circle the soft-lit centerpiece.
When she finds the soundtrack to a movie
I haven't seen and extends her arm and sings along,
I dance back-up, shuffling side to side.

Frances Ann Crowley

Fiction

Christmas Eve 1958
Heav'n and Nature Sing

Jack rode through the yard with the tiny Holstein held in front of him on the saddle. The mama cow—the kids had named her Tootsie—was following behind, bellowing all the way. He didn't want his kids treating livestock as if they were pets, but now, even he was calling the young milk cow "Tootsie."

Tootsie wasn't with the other cows that afternoon, when they were herded to the barn. While the hired man finished the evening chores, Jack rode out to look for her. He found her, not far away, under a cutbank along the river. She had dropped her calf near the thin ice at the river's edge. This cow had been orphaned at birth a couple of years back and had been nothing but trouble since then. He hoisted the calf onto the saddle, mounted up, and headed for home.

After getting the cow and her calf settled in a stall and taking care of his horse, Jack left the barn and crossed the footbridge. A few fat snowflakes were falling. There was no wind. And the stars—how about those stars? He was chilled and bone-weary, but the night was just getting started. There was the twenty-mile drive to church, the candlelight service, and then they would stop at his wife's parents for a short visit. The kids were already Christmas-wild.

Jack would have liked to have stayed in the cow-warmed barn for a while. He loved the smells of sweet hay and saddle leather and he wanted to watch Tootsie and her calf get to know each other. He thought about the shepherds—the "rednecks" of Bethlehem. They were his favorite part of the manger scene.

As soon as he entered the kitchen, the kids, who had been at the window when he rode through the yard with Tootsie trailing behind him, wanted to know if they could go to the barn and see the baby. His wife frowned when he told them they could run down to the barn and take a quick peek. He knew he would catch hell later.

When the kids returned from the barn, the family got ready and hurried to the car. Jack figured if he drove a bit faster than usual, they could make it to the church just in time for the service. As the old Chevy bumped along on icy gravel, he glanced up. The sky was velvet and the stars were doing their Christmas best. For once, there was no noise coming from the back seat.

Jack breathed deeply and relaxed his shoulders. It had been a rough day. He knew, in the year to come, there would be others, but for this one moment, all was calm.

James Bettendorf

Honorable Mention Poetry

Lake House

Be sure you lift the seat when you use the toilet
(she knew her boys), *and put it down when you're done,*
she said when we arrived at the lake.

It was an outhouse. At my friend's cabin we fished,
rowed the boat around, swam for hours and peed
in the lake. We ate hot dogs and chips,

we bedded down in the loft. In the middle
of the night, I woke to the sounds of card playing,
ice rattling in glasses, and quiet laughter.

We can't play strip poker, one of the kids
might wake up. As an adult I think they were kidding
but at twelve years old I began to imagine.

I'd never seen a live naked woman before
so, I fit their faces on pictures I'd seen
followed by a strange wonderful shudder.

In the morning I couldn't look any of them
in the eye and I'm sure they thought
me a quiet, strange, shy child.

Neil Dyer

Poetry

One October Day

Wind is high in the trees
Today, insistent, pressing an
Early snow against
The jack pines and birches,
The deer-colored woods we
Walked through were so still
And white-capped and
There was just the tree tops
Hissing high above us—
The late afternoon
Lake is pouting froth,
Rolling onto the sand
Now skinned in cones
And needles and wood

LeRoy N. Sorenson

Honorable Mention Poetry

The Echo of Her Shout

I remember my mother shouted *I hate you*
as I fled the room, the dark stain
of the eastern sky in sunset.
I remember driving ninety miles per hour
down Highway 14, knuckles white
on the steering wheel.
I remember I could not breathe.
I remember I cried, stopped, then moaned.
I remember the fury in her green eyes,
her face flushed and shiny.
I remember my house cold, so dark,
so empty. I remember my wife returned,
much later, and wrapped herself around me.
I remember, two days later, the 4 a.m. call.
My mother dead.
I remember storm, the bay of northwest wind,
my hands trembling on the drive
to her funeral. The crush of kin around
me, the chunks of tomato soup fed
to them in the church basement.
I remember the hole of her grave.
The echo of her shout.
The day I realized she was really gone.

Dawn Loeffler

Poetry

A Child's Reasoning

Stopped in mid-run
from hallway to kitchen
Darien's gold-streaked green eyes darted
to his younger sister
Brown jagged locks
sweat matted against his forehead
His right arm extended
well beyond the sleeve of his favorite Spiderman sweatshirt
His index finger a laser pointer
directed at her heart
For he knew, even at seven years old
that she was wrong
His voice bounced against the dirty grey walls
echoing into her life
That Is My Dad!
Not Your Daddy!

Kathleen J. Pettit

Creative Nonfiction

Chocolate

I am often dazzled, delighted, and filled with dreams of a special kind of chocolate.

But, chocolate drops do not dance through my head, molten chocolate flourless cake with mounds of fresh vanilla ice cream does not entice me, velvety smooth dark chocolate mousse with a hidden dome of crème brulee resting on a milk chocolate hazelnut praline cookie does not inspire rhapsodic visions for me; Mayan sipping chocolate with classic chocolate truffles adorning a Grand Marnier pound cake smothered with Potion No. 9 Chocolate Sauce garnished with fresh strawberries and raspberries does not send me to the moon. But a piece of my dad's chocolate fudge would make all right with the world.

My dad could not cook. But he could make babies. It was the duty of the daughters to cook when Mom had a baby which was almost every other year. We became very adept at making peanut butter sandwiches, boiled eggs and toast, and cold cereal. And our father, a man with a simple palate, was just fine with this fare. But, come Christmas time, a hunger would descend on him. He needed fudge. He wanted fudge. He dreamed fudge. He was tormented by fudge. So he made fudge. His fudge was dark brown, slightly burnt, grainy and filled with chopped walnuts. Babies teethed on this fudge. Many a child lost teeth trying to eat this fudge. This fudge did not smear all over our fingers or crumble in our hands. It had to be gnawed in order to get the full flavor of it.

Because it was the only thing Dad ever cooked, we devoured it as soon as we could get our hands on it. So Dad hid his fudge. But we always found it, at the back of the highest cupboard, under his pillow, in the garage, under the back seat of the car. At the holidays, finding fudge was our mission. Gifts were only a distraction. As the family grew, one batch of fudge would not do, so Dad cooked more and became creative in his hiding it. He would put a small tin of fudge in an obvious place and the rest in new spots to try to fool us. He even tried hiding the fudge in plain sight.

The game of fudge hide-and-seek went on for many years until one Christmas season, the fudge pan did not make an appearance. Dad, now a grandpa, discovered chocolate kisses. He hid these just as he hid the fudge, only now it was the grandchildren who did the seeking. And they all knew his favorite hiding spot. The minute they entered his house, they ran to his room to find him and his kisses. He would hand them out to his grandbabies with tenderness and a sense that each kiss was a gift as valuable as a pot of gold. You see, it was the only way he ever knew how to say *I love you*.

Jennifer Hernandez

Poetry

Non-renewable Resources

They say green energy
is the future, officials
cutting ribbons for
wind turbines and solar
power plants, energy
never created, just
converted.

My grandfather managed
a rural electric co-op.
They ran wires across
the prairie, lit up farmsteads,
while the furnace in his own home
burned coal, delivered
to the back door and dumped
down a chute into a sooty pile
in the basement.

I have miles of memories
conserved, preserved,
like dill pickles, chokecherry syrups,
strawberry-rhubarb jams on cellar shelves.
When my grandma got Alzheimer's,
they moved her to an apartment in Fargo.
My mom and my aunt found rows
of Mason jars, full of such bounty,
date indeterminate. All thrown out.

Children of the Depression
never got used to having enough.
We who have come of age
in times of abundance
wonder where enough ends
and too much begins.

Susan McMillan

Poetry

Burned

In puckered silence they sit—
him at the head of the table
where he reigns over every meal,
            her at the business end
toward the kitchen, close
in case of boil-overs or burns.

This silence, not the type for kisses
but contrary disconnection, dissension.
She can no longer bend, or stand
for one crumb more of his disdain.
            Biscuits too brown?
            Too bad.

This is a standoff. Stalemate. Gridlock
along the beltline of long-wedded life.
It's long past time he did his share.
            Tomorrow you can cook
            your own damned dinner.

She ignores him as he stews a bit,
pushes away his chair, heads off in a huff.
            She hears the engine start,
truck tires sputter through rain as he rolls out,
leaves her there amid dirty dishes
and acrid emptiness.

She's tired of him in his rage,
his impossible expectations.
She rises, gathers the uneaten biscuits.
            I'll lop off their burned bottoms,
            serve them again for breakfast.

Marlys Guimaraes

Creative Nonfiction

Breakfast

I hold my Raggedy Ann doll close, filter her red yarn hair through my fingers. The bedroom is cold. I'm encased in heavy blankets to keep heat from escaping my slight body. I hear a low whistle coming from the kitchen.

"Mama's happy today," I tell Raggedy.

I imagine her standing at the stove in her yellow shirtwaist dress, its gathered skirt hugging a tiny waist, her jet-black hair curled around her face.

I can smell she's making those fried eggs that are so crispy she has to scrape their edges gently with a spatula to loosen them from the pan.

I stroll into the kitchen and get onto my red stool, feeling a blast of cold air when Dad comes in the back door, stamping clinging snow off his shoes. He ruffles my brother's hair.

In the corner, my sister bangs her spoon on the high chair. We sit at the table, Dad says grace, Mom dishes out bacon and eggs. Just as I am biting into a slice of buttered homemade toast, Dad announces, "Mom, I think it's time to move again."

I look at Mom, her fork suspended in mid-air, and I knew it would be a long time before I heard her whistle again.

Audrey Kletscher Helbling

Poetry

Final Harvest

The cornstalk rises tall, straight
from the pink five-gallon bucket
set next to an uncomfortable tan chair
on carpet the color of dirt.

If the retired farmer in the wheelchair
looks long enough, he imagines rows of corn
rooted in a field of rich black soil,
leaves unfurling under a wide blue sky.

Staff stops to check the corn plant
seeded on May 13, not too late,
says the old farmer as he pours water
into the bucket, soaking the soil.

I focus my camera lens on the cornstalk,
pleased and amused by its placement here
like a still life shadowing beige walls
in the community room of my mom's care center.

Adrian S. Potter

Creative Nonfiction

Storm Warning

Ask her for a story and the narrative unfurls like a spool of ribbon. How she clutched hope like a stuffed animal until bad weather passed, huddled inside a storm shelter, body heat steaming over lanterns and dusty canning jars. Each summer, the winds came back around and blew through town like drifters ready to deliver chaos again. The somber wreckage of gas stations and lampposts hopelessly bent into vees, sycamores snapped like matchsticks. The lightning that flickered nervously through cracks in the cellar door. Her father perched on the top stair, hands wrapped tightly around the handle. Who'd have known she was open raw to the rainfall and squalls, the hatch of her mouth birthing things worse than catastrophe? Testimonials of how rebuilding can become so routine that you anticipate it, how pain sometimes lasts longer than the wound that invents it.

Joel Van Valin

Honorable Mention Poetry

We Stripped Off Our Wet Clothes

We stripped off our wet clothes
and hooked the hangers on the pipes
then crept up the rain-enclosed stairs
and up another flight

naked, and sat in the kitchen
drinking spiced rum and listening
to an old radio show while children
walked home from school in the spring.

The sheets were cool with wisdom
but there was that mud in my hair
and your eyes looked so dark in the bedroom
and spring like a soothsayer

rang out in my ears, saying *This
is spring, a season unlike all others
for a beautiful girl is in love with your kiss
and you can't get enough of her!*

And resting my head on your shoulder
I felt I was dead and laid to rest . . .
so we hardly heard the dryer buzzer
telling us to get dressed.

Sharon Harris

Creative Nonfiction

Performance Art

I am attending the Billiards National Singles Championship in Las Vegas. Over a hundred pool tables are spread out in one huge room and countless pool players are playing or observing, mesmerized.

The players are tense and nervous. They circle the table, calculating the next shot and the next and the next. They see many plays ahead, bending down, lining up, thinking, planning, considering. They know not only which pocket the next ball must roll into, but also how they can touch the cue ball so exactly that it knows whether to roll ahead or come back to them to line up for the next planned shot. This is called English, that precise control of the cue ball.

I appreciate their skill, these pool players who dedicate themselves to perfection, to the scrutiny of the lie of the table. They believe that if they only study it long enough, they can run each table. They can plan far in advance and they are willing to spend hour upon hour in windowless basements or dark smoky bars. They stretch and bend and reach, playing endless games, learning the movements of the cue ball.

I follow one well-known player as he works through the games, winning and winning, moving up the brackets. Loud music plays around him, people drink and talk and laugh. His focus is intense. He talks with no one. He sees only the expanse of green felt that is his world.

Decisions made, he steps to the edge of the table and finds his stance. Like an artist, he performs.

I'd like to tell him: I love watching you as your eyes flicker over the table, seeing the angles, knowing the invisible paths you will follow. I love watching you slip into the zone. I know that a white noise is all you can hear; the table top is all you can see. That revered mental place is yours; right now you cannot miss. Your expensive cue stick slides easily between your fingers. The powdered tip intimately taps the cue ball. A puff of powder floats into the intense light above the table, drifting with the smoke, the music, the tension in the air. The object ball glides smoothly into the pocket. The cue ball responds to your touch and backspins to the spot you need it to be, as if it had no other option.

Much later, I take my leave. I will take those moments with me and remember my response to his touch, his magic, his control.

Lane Rosenthal

Poetry

Pas de Deux

We danced
together you and I
hips swaying to
a beat

only we could hear

as sparks flew
fireworks from your eyes
and your smile lit
the night.

Dawn Loeffler

Honorable Mention Poetry

She Gracefully Stepped Aside

Upon entering the room
he told me there was no rush
no reason I was called
But in his every movement there was:
urgency
agitation
sentiment
water-glazed eyes
all the ingredients of goodbye
So, I kissed her hollow translucent cheek
and whispered, "I love you"
just before alarms announced her departure
The room filled instantly
lights, noise, people
rushing past each other
hell-bent to make her stay
But I knew she was smiling at the chaos
with that "what if" look
just like when she brought up alternative options to my fairy tales
or questioned my boyfriends about their future housekeeping goals
or when I, pregnant at eighteen, said, "Well, that's it,"
she said, "Well, what if You Can do it all,"
or, like she just might trip someone rushing past just to see
if I might giggle
for she loved me too

Laura Krueger-Kochmann

Poetry

Playing Favorites

a child's question

my choice
in less than an instant
an instinct

the berries in my oatmeal bowl
health and color

the big jay outside in the feeder
boldly scaring the little birds away

soft, worn jeans
fraying at the hems

wild lupine
growing along the highway

my daughter's eyes
and mine
in the mirror

the glassy liquid
rippling along the tip of our canoe
and above dense green land
its twin
a bright openness with a few wispy clouds

it could be
water or sky

Ryan M. Neely

Fiction

A Page from the Diary of Ferdinand: Feline Protector of Humanity

We may have lost these humans. Their apostasy has never been more apparent than now, the slow, dark days of winter.

Each morning the humans under my watch abandon the warmth of our snuggle long before dawn. They grumble against the cold and decry a lack of sleep but still they shuffle to the adjacent den where they have erected a shrine to their new gods.

The shrine is a squat, multi-tiered pedestal upon which rests the instrument of these new gods: the magic window.

Despite the dark hour and their own protestations, my humans stroke the shrine, speak to it until it illuminates and speaks back. In a ritual that might seem familiar, the humans dance and gyrate and sweat before the shrine. They mimic the movements of the gods there as if begging for favors or forgiveness.

None of it makes sense. Perhaps they ask for the return of the long days of summer. Perhaps it's forbidden knowledge they seek. Perhaps they demand sustenance for their family, a request I would endorse as they consider me such.

For an hour, my humans mimic the movements of the gods within the shrine. Then, just as they've exhausted themselves, the gods in the magic window disappear and my humans drop to the floor, distraught.

They prostrate themselves before the magic screen, bowing and twisting their bodies, obviously begging the gods to return.

But they do not. Not right away. Instead, the magic screen displays images of faraway places. Lands my humans may never see.

My job is to protect my humans, to keep them from straying to these false gods. During their supplications, I weave myself between their legs. The figure eight pattern of infinity to ward them against evil from the magic window. When they lie with their faces on the floor, I press my third eye into theirs so the bond between us will help them to see the light. Every position in which they contort their bodies during their moment of prayer gives me the chance to wend my way around them, casting spells of protection and of wisdom.

It is uncertain if any of it works. My powers alone may not be strong enough to compete against the magic window.

My humans turn to the shrine once more at dusk. The visions it offers are harder to compete against. Glimpses into the homes of other humans, watching how they hurt and forgive one another. Visions of terrible futures where humans leave Earth (and us) behind. Images of my brethren brainwashing humans into thinking we have no purpose beyond entertaining them. Making them laugh.

Worst of all, however, is the very thing that may be draining my powers and my ability to keep my humans from falling prey to the gods of the magic window. It occurs during the hours between dawn and dusk. Daylight. When the sun is out and dark magic should be at its weakest, the gods of the magic window work their powers on me.

When the humans under my care depart for the day, the magic window has convinced them to leave its gods active. The cursed thing taunts me with phantom birds and squirrels frolicking in the summer sun. Several times it has lulled me into believing they were real and I am ashamed to admit I pounced upon a rodent or fowl hoping the flesh would restore my magic, hoping its carcass would ward this home only to have my nose smashed in and my brain concussed. A bruised forehead and a bruised ego are all I have to show for my vigilance against this unreality—bruises and the echoing laughs of my humans when they discovered the origin of my pain.

I must redouble my efforts to protect them, to bring them back to the salvation of the old ways, but I fear I am not strong enough. Perhaps, one day, others will join my cause but until then I stand ever vigilant and sing the song of our people—a chant of mewls and meows loud enough to scare the dead—to distract my humans from these false gods.

Jennifer Jesseph

Poetry

Big, Fat Poetry

Oh, my poems are flabby and gabby now. They're no longer sleek, fit,
and tight, but
heavier, richer, and robust. I trust my word flow and let it go.

I suppose I could try stuffing them into some smaller,
starker stanzas
to slim
the word count.

I could cut them down to the fine bones of a honed, toned, youthful
poem, like a sprinter
on its mark with chiseled muscles, taut, and ready to pounce.

But I won't. No thanks. No girdles or Spanx for my overweight, wordy
poems.
I'll take the heavy words, all their pounds and various sounds and let
them waddle free
on the page.

Some younger, thinner poet will craft sleek, slender lines. Those used to
be mine.
Those poems can sprint to the finish. They'll be the winner, the new
writing wonder,

while I will blunder and barrel along with my curvy songs. I'll be with my
words spilling
and filling up pages.

Let my poems be great with wonder. Let them be voluminous and
billowy.
Let my writing be fat. It has thickened with age and renders me in
middle sage.

Oh large, lovely words!
You are home. You are home
in this fleshy, plump, and meaty poem.

Kristin Laurel

Poetry

Pond Affair

Morning sunlight
casts color
to the rocks
where the leopard frog sits
at the water's edge
for hours
with bulging eyes,
wet, leafy-green skin
until, finally, he jumps—
plop.

All afternoon,
he sits
in the water,
his eyes and nose
above the surface
drinking and breathing
through his skin.

At dusk,
after my bath,
I sit on the porch, listening
to his amorous ribbits;
smiling, I take a sip of wine,
blinking my eyes
when I swallow.

Anne Stewart

Poetry

Winter Moon

High as a mid-June sun, the winter moon
illuminates snow, lays shadow forest
on glazed, white ground, the muted night
quiescent.

Great Gray stretches wings wide:
soundless, adumbral form moving
swiftly over frozen surface tracking a vole
hidden beneath snow.

Silhouetted, a flying squirrel
launches from high pine branch, glides
to feeder on my window's sill, lands with a thump
absorbed into the hush of light.

Kristin Laurel

Poetry

Little Blue Heron

I walk over to the river, walk past
the empty tent, where a homeless man
sleeps under the bridge
at night; I walk past the rotting
tire thrown in with the current. Bikes race
past me, cars swish by, but midway
over the bridge, I stop:

A slate-blue statue stands
at the river's edge,
wading with stick legs,
yellow eyes peering.
I find myself holding
my breath, until finally,
he tiptoes a few steps,
dips his sharp beak into
the water and comes up
with a cream-colored snake.

He looks toward the sky,
his long neck stretches,
as he clamps down his beak
and slowly engulfs
his moving piece of spaghetti.

Little Blue Herons are born white,
and turn grayish-blue as they mature.
I wonder if it took him a while, too,
to learn to stand strong,
                              to wait.

A Holiday Weekend

"What is the speed limit here?" he asked.

"I think it's eighty," she said.

Their car idled dead-still behind an 18-wheeler rig with an East Coast license plate. Sunlight radiated off the tar. The stopped traffic of both northbound lanes of the Interstate Highway System revved their engines like shivering nerve ends.

"There isn't one road in all of Minnesota with a speed limit of eighty." He took his eyes off the highway to look at her. "Are you drunk?"

"Maybe a little." She yawned. "I painted this morning and forgot to open a window." She brought her hand up for him. A different rainbow color glossed each of her fingernails.

"Are all of the bridesmaids wearing those?" He looked back to the road.

She nodded.

"They're like Christmas bulbs," he said.

They laughed.

Their vehicles rolled forward from time to time. The couple won minutes of shade as they met one of the rare underpasses that far north of The Cities. Then, back in the sun, a second semi-trailer crept along the driver's side door and stopped.

"I am in a box," said the man. He began to sweat. "Can you see anything?"

She stared into the back end of the East Coast semi-trailer rig. Her face sagged.

He took his eyes off the road to look at her. "I think this car is filling with diesel exhaust. Why don't we fix the air conditioner?" He turned the dashboard dial for no reason.

They moved up the highway like multi-ton hewn stones.

"It's the cabin people driving up early," he said, almost to himself.

"No." She shook her head. "There can't be this many cabin people on a Thursday morning."

"It's three-thirty in the afternoon."

Her mouth widened. She fumbled her smartphone from the purse by her feet. "But who gets married on a Thursday, anyway?" She said it almost to herself. "And why at a lake resort?"

The man reached across to the passenger side and took the smartphone from her hand. "What are you doing?"

"I'm going to call." She considered her next words. "We'll be late."

"No." He set the phone into her lap and took her hand. "We might make it."

Wafts of melting tar. The grumble of stalled traffic and a grittiness in the teeth. Three crows danced around a tuft of roadkill. "Caw! Caw! Caw!"

"There." The woman gestured out her side window. They scrolled past a seventy-mile-per-hour road sign stuck to the concrete barricade.

"Ha!" It came out of him like a cough. "There is no road anywhere in the state of Minnesota that would let you drive eighty miles an hour."

She yawned.

"There!" she said.

He startled from a daze.

Traffic merged out of the right lane and the man maneuvered his car to the left between the two semi-rigs. Tilting on the highway's shoulder, a motorcycle had run up the end of a small pick-up truck and lodged to a stop deep into the back window of the cab. The drivers of the machines lay in a ditch hidden behind rows of arriving emergency medical people and their vehicles.

She shuddered. "How fast was he going to get up there like that?"

"Fast," he said.

"Do you think he'll live?" She pressed the rainbow fingertips of one hand to her mouth.

"No," he said. "None of them."

At eighty miles an hour, as traffic broke loose from the accident scene, the man passed the 18-wheeler rig with the East Coast license plate. The bluster of speed cleared the car of fumes and stagnant heat. The woman returned the smartphone to her purse. The man rested his elbow out the open window and pressed the accelerator.

Peggy Trojan
Poetry

Marriage Bed

I sleep in half-wasted bed,
you in memory care,
I in my new apartment.

I stay on my own side,
having learned over six decades
what boundaries are.

Susan Niemela Vollmer

Poetry

Neighbor

She putters in her yard
Lining up the resin statues like some graveyard scene
The newest flowers are brightly fake cemetery bouquets
She hangs and re-hangs the pots of real flowers
Aggressively mows the lawn and slices down the weeds

I wonder if this is her therapy
Exorcising or appeasing the demons of drugs and alcohol
The memories of the murderer and arsonist who was her partner
Her nights in jail after being dragged screaming from the house
The hysterical rise in her voice as she scolded her children

Perhaps there is a sense of comfort that comes
From the symmetry of a neatly mown lawn
From the soothing sound of a stream of water into a flower pot
Faith in the climbing of a vine or the hue of a blossom
Hope that imitation will give rise to real peace

Meridel Kahl

Poetry

Vigil

I stand at the kitchen window
watching the setting sun
brush treetops with gold
listening to beluga-like calls
of the lake as it makes ice
when a bird hits the French door
with a dull, flat thud.
She drops, stunned,
onto the front deck,
her eyes wary, glazed slits,
her body a handful of plumped-up
brown and cream feathers.

For two hours I gather
giant swathes of hope
wrap them around
a body weighing less than an ounce
focus on the frantic beat
of a tiny, four-chambered heart
until its rhythm proves faithful enough
to open her wings
guide her safely
to the branches of a nearby oak
this cold December evening.

Linda Maki

Poetry

The Slippers

Your old brown slippers
rest on the bathroom floor,
waiting for you to come home.

Year by year the heels wore
down, measuring restless
nights, lazy football Sundays.

You have danced in them, paced
fussy babies in your arms, even run
through snow after a runaway puppy.

The night your dad died
you wore them to the hospital
with an overcoat and jeans.

Tonight, I reach down, take them
up, crush them to my chest
with reverence.

Bernadette Hondl Thomasy

Honorable Mention Creative Nonfiction

Mother's Mojo

Like all the condolences, the sympathy message was well-intentioned. "You'll always have your mother with you," the card assured me. That sounded comforting but my heart still felt crushed at the loss of my mother. I was spoiled; Mom had been there for all of my seventy-three years. But it wasn't long enough.

I could not accept the fact that I would never hear her voice again on our twice-a-week phone calls. There would be no cards. No two-week visits to my home and to hers. I felt sad, unfocused, had no appetite and no desire to take care of my own family.

One day, weeks later, I found the energy to prepare sloppy joes for dinner. As I browned the ground beef and added the chopped onion and celery, the aroma of the familiar ingredients prompted memories of Mom stirring and stirring this family-favorite food. I felt like she was standing beside me, reminding me, "simmer the beef and vegetables slowly, it takes time." I get it now, that's why her sloppy joes tasted so amazing. Mom had learned patience in cooking and in life. She chewed her food slowly, enjoying all the flavor and texture. She was usually the last one eating at a meal. "What's your hurry?" she'd ask us. Indeed, what was so important we couldn't take time to appreciate food and each other?

My two sisters felt the loss of Mom as deeply as I did, perhaps, even more so because they both lived closer. Like other families when the last parent passes, we survivors faced a myriad of financial and legal details. As we worked together to sort things out, we arranged a call with our lawyer. And I experienced another heart-felt Mom moment. After each of us was connected on the call, my older sister came on and said, "Hi, Berna." I could not believe what I heard; surely it was my mother speaking my family nickname. I had never noticed the similarity between my sister's and mother's voices. On that day, I knew Mom was there with us on the phone.

Another post-funeral task involved sorting through boxes of saved memorabilia. There wasn't a birthday or Valentine's card Mom didn't treasure. As I studied the handwriting on messages that I had sent to her over the years, I was confused. Was that my handwriting or Mom's? It seems my compact, but legible cursive script was morphing into my mother's handwriting, a pattern I had noticed years earlier between two of my nieces and their mother. Some say we become our parents. Perhaps that is how we keep them close.

David LeCount

Poetry

The Sweater

There would come a time when you wished you knew better

That elderly aunt who, every Christmas, knitted you a sweater

Some day when you're old enough

You'll take that old sweater off the shelf

Then though it protects you from the cold

The real warmth is from the love she put in every stitch that she sewed

Of all the games and toys

That excite little boys

How many are still here

Kept for all these years?

But now that you're elderly yourself,

There's always been love in your house to this day

Because the love she put in every stitch never went away

Steven R. Vogel

Poetry

White Pines

This back eighty has been logged off,
and only scrub and pulp remain.
They may as well be weeds,
grown up as they are through the
moonshine hoops and into the cabin
no one could find.

Nothing but hazel, ivy, a few box elders,
maybe a couple of maples among
the poplars, mostly poplars and jacks.

There is a slight rise just off
the hogsback. You can smell it more
than see it from the trail, but just go
over there once. You will find
a few reds and a couple of whites—
forgotten items, if you don't know.

Seedlings when the axe fell, you would
think. But they're too old—too old
to be made little, too old to play odd.

See? We didn't take it all.
We did what you promised should be
in this wood after the still was shattered,
when the whites bled themselves out
and left those reds and a clump
of birches worshiping by the lake.

Christine J. Grossman

Poetry

Christmas at Fort Ripley State Cemetery

Your grave
Seems so far
Away—
"Mom always
Hated
To be cold,"
Reminisced Sis.
The house would
Be heated to
85 degrees.
(Highest heat bill
In the neighborhood.)
Now she lies
Blanketed
("lies blanketed":
How cliché.)
Under two
(or three)
Feet of
Snow.
You're
There
With her.
It's where you'd
Want
To be.
But it leaves me
As lonely as
The deserted
Snowy
Street
Outside
My
Window.

Marlene Mattila Stoehr

Poetry

Farm Home Supper

Seventy years married, most evenings
Anna fried potatoes in homemade lard
for herself and Ernie.
This night she fries for three—
her son, herself, and me.

She chops at sizzling slices
with her trusty aluminum spatula
(a premium from the feed store)
and steadies the wobbly handle
of the Priscilla Ware frying pan.

From my vantage point I muse upon
the circle of life, and note that the
curve of Anna's aged spine is echoed
in the matching curve of her bent
and long-serving frying pan.

Victoria Lynn Smith

Honorable Mention Fiction

Cora Comes to an Understanding

"It's 72," I say, after peeking at the thermometer outside the backdoor. I write the temp on the chalkboard hanging by the window overlooking Grandpa Harold's gigantic garden.

"Needs to be 74 by one o'clock," Grandma Cora says, "otherwise it's too cold for swimming." She wipes her nose and shoves a hanky back into her apron pocket, putting an exclamation point on her words.

And if it reaches 74 after that, she won't take us because she's got to can and freeze stuff that comes out of Grandpa's garden. He gives her updates every morning. Yesterday, he said, "Cora, there's peas need shelling." This morning he said, "Cora, the beans need picking."

Between all that canning and freezing, she's baking bread, cookies, cakes, and pies. Grandpa doesn't like store-bought bread, and I think he declared a law that his meals must have dessert. Then, she's got to cook supper before Grandpa gets home from the gas station he owns.

A week ego, instead of filling his plane with skydivers, Dad loaded up Christina and me and flew us to our grandparents. Mom had surgery the week before and almost died. To save her, the doctors cut her open from her navel to her private parts. Being my sister's nine and I'm ten, no one told us any of that, but they didn't have to because we did some eavesdropping. Grandma met us at the small airport near her home. Dad stashed our luggage into her station wagon and said, "You girls behave yourselves." As Grandma drove away, I watched Dad start his pre-flight check before he flew back home.

We've been here a week now and Grandma has us trapped in her routine. We eat breakfast and do the dishes. We eat lunch and do the dishes. We eat supper and do the dishes. Between meals we play outside or walk to the IGA and buy penny candy when Grandpa gives us each a dime. If the temp's warm enough by one o'clock, Grandma takes us swimming. After, she has to hustle to get her chores done and supper cooking.

Today, our thermometer-watching started while we set the table for lunch.

"You're going to let all the flies in," Grandma snarls. "You don't need to check the temperature every five minutes. It's either going to be 74 or not."

She's got a point, but it doesn't stop us.

Grandma goes to church every Sunday and plays the organ and leads the choir. Dad says that she's a God-fearing, praying woman. I believe she prays every day the temp won't reach 74. Christina and I aren't church-going, but we pray for rising temps.

The firehouse siren wails, telling us it's noon.

The backdoor opens. "Cora, I just came from the garden. The raspberries need picking too." Grandpa's home for lunch.

"It's 73," Christina says and writes the temp on the chalkboard.

Grandma's shoulders sag, and she sighs.

After lunch, before we can check the temp again, Grandma sends us to the basement with old newspapers, which Grandpa burns in a small stove. When I come up the stairs, I see Grandma's butt holding the backdoor open, and it looks like she's messing with the thermometer. Behind me, Christina belches and startles her.

"That was quick," Grandma says, smoothing her silver-gray hair. She's acting like she always hangs out the back door to fix her hair. Her fingers are wet. I say nothing, but I know the temp has dropped. We aren't going swimming.

Then the phone rings, and Grandma leaves the kitchen to answer it.

I wait until she's all wrapped in her call and open the back door. It's 70 degrees. I place my thumb on the thermometer and watch the red line rise. It hits 75. I go back inside and help Christina finish the dishes. Grandma returns to the kitchen.

Five minutes before one, I hang up my dishtowel and check the temp.

"It's 75." I grin.

"What?" Grandma says.

We look at each other—eyeball to eyeball—a cheater's standoff.

After we get home from swimming, Grandma picks beans and cooks supper. We stay out of her way.

Shortly after five, Grandpa comes home. "Cora, I told you the raspberries needed picking."

"Christina and I are doing that after supper," I say. "We begged Grandma to let you teach us how to pick them."

Grandma and I look at each other—eyeball to eyeball—a liar's agreement.

She smiles first.

Susu Jeffrey

Poetry

Footprints

Shadows
are the footprints
of the sun.

Christopher Mueller

Poetry

Hand Over Hand

Afternoon has entered the forest
like a deer leaping onto a road,
and the gray light of the clouds
stares at you through the leaves
and looks into the clear water
the way you might look into your memory
and see your mother.

She would have climbed this tree
when she was younger,
hand-over-hand up to the high branches
where her own mother wouldn't see her
and she could look out for miles and miles
at the quiet afternoon
and fly anywhere she liked.

Audrey Kletscher Helbling

Creative Nonfiction

A Quick Guide to Practicing Minnesota Nice

Leave the last bar in the cake pan.

Encourage the mom with the screaming toddler at Target because you were once her.

Shovel snow from your neighbor's driveway even if your back hurts like hell.

Rather than state outright that you don't like something, say, "That's different."

Buy a ticket to every pancake breakfast fundraiser in town.

Pick up folding chairs after a contentious church meeting which started and ended in prayer.

Don't pretend to like lutefisk, but respect those who do.

Share your surplus zucchini with anyone who will take them.

Accept surplus zucchini when you already have plenty, just to be nice.

Talk about the weather because to do otherwise would appear un-Minnesotan.

Scoop up candy at a parade and give all of it, even the chocolate, to the kids next to you.

Dress up when you'd rather wear jeans and a Paul Bunyan buffalo plaid shirt.

Root for the Vikings, believing they may just make it to the Super Bowl this year.

Root for the Twins, believing they may just make it to the World Series this year.

Buy local, not because it's trendy, but because you appreciate a hardware store in town.

Thank garage sale customers, even if they've bought nothing, because, hey, they stopped.

Wave other drivers ahead at a four-way stop to avoid any

appearance of being in a hurry.

Secretly embrace roundabouts as the best thing since sliced bread.

Watch a high school football play-off game in thirty-degree temps because you can handle the cold.

Claim you love Tater Tot Hotdish when you prefer Chicken Wild Rice Casserole.

Buy tickets to a Meat Raffle after you've just picked up a quarter of beef from the locker.

When friends flee to Florida in February, finagle a visit without appearing too eager.

Finally, smile, and, as Mom advises, "Just be nice."

Vincent O'Connor

Poetry

Priorities

sorry I missed your call,
but I was weeding my garden
and the morning sun
seduced me

Julie Martin

Poetry

Cove Point, Two Harbors

Cobble to cobble,
boulder to boulder,
we pick our way

The reverie is pierced—

to the water's edge
to watch the day
melt into the lake.

swarms of mosquitoes descend
intoxicated
by the carbon dioxide cocktail

A thin stripe of pink
hovers over the tops
of evergreen, aspen, and birch.

of our breath
followed by
a bombardment of dragonflies

On an outcrop of basaltic lava flow,
billions of years old,
eroded by water, we sit

who blitz around our heads,
obliterate mosquitoes midflight,
deliver us into

and wait
for the waning gibbous moon
to make its appearance.

a twilight that glints
from wings to water
to feldspar crystals.

As waves crash against the shore,
rocks clatter and chatter,
chiming, lulling, hypnotic.

Christopher Mueller

Poetry

Fishing

The lake has taken
my lure and pulled it deep.
I've lost track of my artifice
and tricks way down in the cold.

I wait on the surface in this boat,
watching the cloudless sky
and the long mirage of the shore.

Nothing happens.

There is nothing left out here—
the perpetual water, the brazen blue.

I've been disintegrated into a chaos
of shallow waves.

In some maybe future the sun will reach its zenith
and perhaps the eagle will launch from the pines.

But now there is no one and nothing
but a ripple of morning light,
the bright color of bliss
shattered on the breeze.

Mike Lein

Fiction

The Locals

The door of the Buckhorn Bar swung open, allowing a blast of below-zero backwoods air to sweep down my side of the bar. The crowd sitting on the far side, Chumlie, Beak, Steinie, and Ronnie, swung their heads in unison, looking up from warming tap beers to see what came with it.

Four kids followed the cold blast in, slamming the door behind them before taking time to survey the surroundings. Two couples, maybe in their thirties but hard to say given their shiny puffy coats and faux fur hats. Each one clutched a smart phone and now surveyed the tight confines of the Buckhorn with wide eyes, suddenly aware of the silence that greeted them.

It was a classic stare-down, like from an old western movie. Someone had to make a move, say the first word. One of the guys finally appointed himself "Leader" and walked forward. The others hung back, nervously looking at us, the ratty stuffed moose head hanging on the wall, and the ancient stuffed muskie decaying below it. Then one of the ladies noticed Big Louie and pointed with a mixture of surprise and horror.

Big Louie sat in an old webbed lawn chair on a shelf above the fuzzy TV. He had been a clothing store mannequin somewhere in a former life. There was speculation he was a garage sale purchase dating back to the '70s. He now watched over the bar, beady eyes peering out from under a hillbilly-style floppy hat, dressed in bibs and lumberjack plaid. Laying across his lap was a rusty double-barrel shotgun, clutched in his cold plastic hands, and pointed towards the far wall—for now.

Butch finished shoving a couple chunks of oak into the blazing fireplace and walked back to reclaim his throne behind the bar. He took a sip of his own beer and stared back at Leader Guy, waiting. We all watched and kept our mouths shut, anticipating what was going down.

Leader Guy blinked and went first—"We're out looking for my

sister. We were supposed to meet her at the place down the road but she didn't show up. You guys seen her here?"

Butch took another sip of beer. "Nope," he said, not bothering to ask for a description. After all, a lone female stepping into the Buckhorn on a winter Saturday night would have been an event talked about for years.

"Well, okay," said Leader Guy, glancing back at his uneasy followers, nervously scrolling their phones, glancing up once in a while to keep an eye on Big Louie. "Maybe she will show up. We might as well have a drink. You got any 'Fireball' whiskey?"

"Nope," said Butch, not bothering to point to the row of half-full bottles of Jack, Jim, Canadian, and Crown on the shelf behind him.

Leader Guy didn't give up. "How about some 'Hot 100'?"

"Nope," said Butch, again letting the bottles behind him speak for themselves.

Leader Guy seemed slow to take a hint. "Well, got anything with some cinnamon to warm us up?"

"Nope," said Butch, sticking to his story.

Leader Guy looked down at his own phone, then started a slow walk backwards to his group, still standing only one step into the Buckhorn. "Well, okay then, I guess we should keep on looking for my sister, don't know where she be, might have to run back to the cabin and check, thanks for the info!"

Butch nodded in return as the group hurried out the door, trying to cram through two at time, again filling the Buckhorn with cold country air. Silence reigned, except for the oak crackling in the fireplace. Butch took a sip of beer and walked over to check the fire.

I tilted my empty glass as he came back. He refilled it with bubbly goodness from the tap and scratched around in the change laying on the bar in front of me. Since things were kinda slow on my side of the bar, I picked up the glass and walked over to the other side to see what wisdom could be found there.

Ronnie greeted me with a laugh and got the conversation rolling again. "Hey guys, remember that night back in the '70s when we had a lottery to shoot the TV when Howard Cosell came on Monday Night Football? That Son-Of-A-Bitch hated the Vikings! Beak—you won the lottery didn't you? Damn that was crazy! I bet ol' Louie is still deaf!"

Peggy Trojan
Poetry

All Relative

"I wish I was sixty-five again,"
I whined in my seventies.

"I know what you mean,"
Pa agreed,
pushing ninety-nine.
"I wish I was eighty-five again."

J. M. S. Swanson

Poetry

Benson Lake

The winter in Benson Lake
settles the spray of spring, hides the mirror of summer,
and captures every autumn leaf-boat that dared to set sail.

In the winter, Benson Lake
is silent save for a song of air gurgling under ice
and the subtle slump when snow slides off shoreline cedars.

Benson Lake in the winter
charts an animal's map of explorations
stories more enticing than humans remember how to tell.

Larry Ellingson
Fiction

Crossing the Bar

The two friends shook hands in front of the downtown café.

"Morning, Ben, good to see you again."

"You too, Hank. It's been a while."

They walked inside and slid into their usual booth. The server came and they ordered coffee. "So, how are you doing?" Ben asked.

"Not great. It's been almost six months since Annie died and . . . it was a shock, of course. It happened so quickly. It was like stepping into complete darkness from a brightly lit room . . . dazed, confused, you know?"

"Yeah, I'm sorry, Hank. It must be hard."

"Mmmm . . . one of the hardest things is looking out the window and seeing the damn boat sitting in the backyard. It feels like it just gets bigger and heavier every time I look at it. I hate the damn thing. It's a curse."

The server put the coffee in front of them and they sipped in silence.

"So why did you get it?" his friend asked.

"I bought it about six years ago, before we retired. I found it in one of those ship graveyards. It was my retirement dream. I would fix it up and Annie and I would sail the Great Lakes . . . anchor in quiet little bays and visit those quaint harbor towns up and down the shore."

"That sounds idyllic. What shape was it in?"

"It had some problems. The propeller and shaft were bent and her sails were mildewed and rotted, but the hull was sound and the engine still worked. She's a twenty-seven foot Catalan, which are common, and I figured I could find parts pretty easily. I knew she would handle nicely . . . very stable . . . shit, the keel weighs a ton."

"You put a lot of work into it?"

"Yeah, I replaced the prop, stripped and repainted the hull and got new sails. But I kept finding other problems. Part of the foredeck and the bulkhead below it were rotting and the electrical and navigation systems needed to be replaced.

"Annie . . . you know Annie; every time I found another issue she worried and fretted over the expense. I don't think she was entirely sold on the idea in the first place."

"I'm sure she would have loved it."

"Maybe. So when she got sick, I kept working on it, thinking that she would get better. I used to sit next to her and show her the charts of the Lakes, where we would go, the best shelter if a storm came up, rocks and bars we'd have to avoid." Hank raised his cup to his lips and held it with two hands. "She crossed the bar without me."

Ben looked away. "Where did you learn to sail?" he finally asked.

"I grew up near a harbor town on the Upper Peninsula. I had a little Sunfish that I would take out into the bay." Hank looked past his friend toward the window and the brightening street. "I even sailed out onto the lake sometimes, tacking and then turning home, coming in so fast and leaning so hard that my head almost touched the water. It was terrifying and thrilling at the same time. It made me feel totally alive. I've never felt anything like that before or since."

They were quiet for a time and then Hank put his cup down. "I've probably been talking too much," he said. "Besides, I just thought of something I need to do."

Ben shook his head. "You weren't talking too much; we have a lot to catch up on."

Hank nodded and slid out of the booth. They shook hands again and Hank walked out into the sunshine, pausing a moment to let it warm his face.

He stopped at the hardware store and bought a can of spray paint and a set of stencils. When he got home he walked into his backyard and looked up at the boat covered in its tarp, like an unveiled sculpture. He pulled the tarp back and climbed the scaffold at the aft of the boat. He took out the stencils and taped the letters to the stern, snapped the cover off the paint and sprayed it cleanly and evenly across the stencil.

When he was finished, he carefully removed the stencil and got down to examine his work. ANNIE was neatly spaced along the length of the stern. A breeze blew through the tarp, making it billow and flap, like a luffing sail. He grasped the line that held it and pulled it in, feeling the tarp go taut.

Marsha Foss

Poetry

A Feast on the Side of the Road

the deer, hit and still,
attended by a murder of crows
though it was not they
who killed him

the slayer fled
indifferent to the bounty
she left behind

J. M. S. Swanson

Honorable Mention Poetry

Quercus

I never asked to be a human—
I would have made a great oak.
Wearing a robe of snow or veil of rain,
quietly gifting the world my acorns.
I sense the subtle satisfaction of a new leaf
finally brushing against a neighboring tree
after years upon years of my reaching.
I know how rich the rain tastes
when drought is washed away
and the intoxication of sunshine
after clouds have overstayed their welcome.
I now invite the birds to call me their home,
generations of blue jays or waxwings or grosbeaks—
I'm not picky. Come and go, come and grow
as I too grow ever up, ever out
and ever down, ever out
where my roots can sense the tendrils
of my born acorns as they sprout to take my place.
When I stand wise and round and proud,
I hope I will fall to the wind and not saws,
a mighty breath pushing me to rest at last
where my final gift will be *me:*
nurturing the land as habitat and soil,
fulfilled and at peace.

Jennifer Hernandez

Poetry

Hybrids

My father, North Dakota
farm boy, once told me:

Now don't be offended,
but I have a theory
about why your boys
are so tall and healthy.

They're hybrids.

If you want strong cattle,
find two parents
of divergent stock.

My great-grandparents
from Scandinavia,
my husband's from Mexico.
Our boys are strong.

We've planted them firmly
in the richest soil
we can muster,
scan the skyline
for storm clouds,
pray against hail.

Avesa Rockwell

Poetry

Ode to Callouses

O, epidermal armor from the thorn, the flame, the sharp edge,
evidence of routine strumming, holding, banging, rubbing, hauling,
crimping:

you thicken to seal off the world
from the keen endings of nerves.

Like a muscle, you require maintenance,
Constant resistance, or else
you grow soft, like a belly.

Does that mean the default is not indifference, but tenderness?

Our DNA knows nothing
about entropy; new cells set out
to replicate our baby selves.
Only the outer layer learns to resist
rock, wood, and ice.

And why do you form so reliably
beneath my wedding band,
as if to remind me this kind of love
is labor made visible,
evidence of routine strumming, holding, banging, rubbing, hauling,
crimping.

Charmaine Pappas Donovan

Creative Nonfiction

Uncle Bill

I want to miss Bill like I miss my mother or other close relatives who have died. But I missed his death and his funeral while vacationing in Hawaii during the Gulf War when he died. I strain to miss an uncle I barely knew. The few times I spent with him seem as vague as his cigarette smoke, yet he was my mother's brother, a branch on my family tree.

I've seen pictures of my siblings and me perched on our plush green couch, a clear-faced, eye-glassed uncle sitting mildly in the middle of our preschool chicken-poxed faces. Piled into a dusty-looking Plymouth, our family drove to the VA hospital in St. Cloud where we visited Uncle Bill. The three of us ran barefoot through flowered grounds on grass like crushed velvet. He let me hold a trembling guinea pig he cared for there, gently asked me not to squeeze its soft, trembling body. They said he was sick, but mostly he looked tired or worn-out.

After he got out of the hospital, he would drop in on us unexpectedly. He took the long way up north on winding, forested Highway 169. Beer in hand, he would pet our dog, Rocky, say he came by to see how we were doing. He rarely entered the house, just stood in the driveway or on the sidewalk smoking Lucky Strike cigarettes. He leaned against the car while talking, picked tobacco from his tongue between smokes.

Once Bill got married, he brought his wife Sally on his road trips. Her memory was as jumbled as an unassembled jigsaw puzzle. (Probably from all the shock treatments.) Bill did not have depression; he was schizophrenic. While their talk was often as random as a ricochet, they nursed beers and filled ashtrays with cigarette butts. They were large people who shrank our living room with their presence while a blue haze of second-hand smoke swirled around them.

The last time I saw Bill was in Hennepin County court. My ex was summoned to appear for a bench warrant. We sat side-by-side awaiting his turn. A bailiff called my uncle's name. He stood up, looking much like he always did with slicked-back blonde hair, khakis and a plaid, double-pocketed shirt. He stepped to the front of the court, faced the judge and addressed him as "Your Honor." I heard Bill plead his case. He admitted his guilt after seeing the Breathalyzer results, paid a fine and was released to meet with a probation officer.

His demeanor struck me; he could have been a different person. He could have become a lawyer if his sanity hadn't deserted him in early adulthood, if drugs used to treat his mental illness had been better, if he hadn't drunk so much. That day in court, I knew him differently. He was a smart man sidetracked by his disease. In court confusion was nowhere near him—delusion waited, sneaky as blue haze, to waylay Bill somewhere beyond those courtroom doors.

Julia Silverberg Nemeth

Creative Nonfiction

Memory on Fire

When I was a girl, I would wake in the early morning to feed the great furnace in the root-cellar. I remember the old, wooden stairs creaking beneath my dirty slippers. Everything was dirty in that house. I remember the earthy smell of the oiled, dirt floor of the cellar. I would open the metal door to the furnace and its metal hinges groaned ominously. Afraid, I'd look into the shadowy corners of the cellar. But I had to accomplish what I set out to do or the water pipes would freeze. Oh, to see the embers still orange with heat was a delightful sight. It meant I didn't have to start the fire from nothing. I pretended the embers were my children. I fed them shovels of black, sooty coal and large pieces of fragrant oak. My children, once fed, exploded into flames, and I crept my way back up the creaking wooden stairs.

Doris Stengel
Poetry

Elegy for Mike

On a smallish street
in a smallish town,
a flock of children grew.
They claimed the turf
of South 7th Street
as their very own.
From the deep ravine
they called "Big Sev"
to the playgrounds
in the park
they traveled as a crew.
Their mothers never worried,
they knew they were safe,
that old women
in small houses
were keeping them in view.
This luxury of freedom
allowed them to explore,
it let them grow in confidence
it made them who they are.
They formed "a band of brothers"
that lasted through the years.
Now one of them
has met "cruel death"
they gather to mourn,
yet they also gather
to celebrate a childhood
of friends who have cared
for each other
to the very end.

Tara Flaherty Guy

Creative Nonfiction

Lifespan, Lovespan

Driving down the main street of my rural lake town last week, I chanced upon a poignant tableau. A Canada goose sat in hopeful watch next to his fatally injured mate near the storm sewer grate. As I drove past them, I saw him get up and waddle around her inert form in a ragged circle. His long black neck and head with its white chinstrap was inclined down in forlorn, mute inquiry toward her body as he circled her. In my rear-view mirror I saw him settle back down in his original posture of patient vigil, his anxious circumnavigation of his dying mate complete for the moment. I know wild geese. I knew he would circle her again and again in his doomed watch until some deep, primeval urge moved him to abandon his faithful post, to take flight, to live on. A wave of sorrow washed over me. Silly to mourn for a bereaved goose, but my grief felt genuine. Having watched in bemusement as modern relationships among family and friends sparked, grew, and died on cold glass screens of one size or another, I found the moment of avian love and loss authentic and touching.

In Minnesota, Canada geese return from the south in the spring, in an arduous, energy-sapping migration home, usually to the same lake, often to the same nesting spot. I knew this as a lifelong lake resident and dispenser of cracked corn, scattered every raw spring to welcome my own flock home. I often wondered if my icy lake was truly home or if home was some unknown warm place in the south. I liked to imagine that since they returned every year to my lake to hatch and raise their goslings, this was home. Despite their peevish, belligerent honking, I thought my lake was home; at least they always came back.

I wondered if the pair had recently nested near the lake in preparation for their eggs before heading out on their ill-fated urban foray. I felt a fresh little spill of sorrow remembering that Canada geese partner for life. With a lifespan that can last twenty-five years, this extraordinary fidelity is singular among waterfowl. *It's rare among my own species, except for a few,* I thought bleakly, my own divorce still raw and new. I thought of my dad, stunned with grief after my mom dropped silently to the kitchen floor one day. Gone forever, his "bride" of forty-eight years. Whether avian or human, sorrow was the bittersweet fate of those left behind when lovespan outstripped lifespan. I wanted to weep for both our species. The geese dwindled to distant specks in my rear-view mirror as the widowed drake sat the last watch for his hen, his life forever changed in an irretrievable moment. I drove on, moved by the tiny, tender testament to faithfulness in the world.

Instructional

She is scolding the vines again,
cigarette to and from her lips,
goose-stepping in a bathrobe, in cold fog.
The morning glories, not yet opened,
have disappointed again—veering off her
corrective placements on twine, porch rail,
trellises. She moves about, chasing light
and shade, annoyed with the inconsistent
offerings of the sun, despite our assurances
that all this is according to order, the plants
knowing well what path to take to make
the most of their short season, flowering
in ecstasy, offering pollen to the caress
of every butterfly and bee, withering, then
blooming, again and again, until the final
turn in autumn when, neither naughty
nor nice, they die according to plan.

Kit Rohrbach

Poetry

Organizing My Sock Drawer

A daguerreotype would do
for most of it—
shades of brown and black.
Only around the edges
does color come:
fuchsia, salmon, yellow, teal,
the green of walking barefoot
through just-mown grass,
fishnets never intended
to catch anything but toes.

Under it all, a photograph
framed, face down,
faded to shades of brown
except around the edges;
the flowers, the grass,
the day we went fishing
and pulled a salmon—
pink-speckled,
wet and shining—
from the water.

Unseen, unforgotten,
hidden safe
beneath the sushi rolls
of my socks.

Kim M. Bowen

Honorable Mention Fiction

The Mangler

My husband and I frequent garage sales in the spring and fall. Once they find we own a resort, often a garage sale host or hostess will mention other items not on display. Twice I've been asked if I'd like to buy a "mangler."

"Uh . . . that sounds monstrous. I'm sorry, I don't know what a 'mangler' is," I said when first asked by a vibrant senior citizen with twinkling blue eyes, a slash of red lipstick, and pink-laced neat, white sneakers.

"It's an iron to press sheets," she answered, in a tone implying, *How can you not know what this is, don't you have one? How do you run a resort without one, dummy?*

"Okay . . . huh. Well, I don't iron the sheets. It takes twelve hours sometimes to wash and fold eighty-one sets of sheets on a Saturday. I can't imagine ironing them, too."

"Back in my day, all resorts had 'em. It was the law," she harrumphed.

"Really?" I felt my insecurities well up, even in a rather innocuous situation. I must be the worst resort owner on the planet. Was I supposed to be ironing sheets? I remembered my grandmother teaching me to iron Grampa's handkerchiefs when I was eight. Like it was a super important life skill she needed to make sure I learned well. Why? The hanky was going to get shoved in his pocket where no one would see it and only be used to wipe snot, right? Gramma ironed everything: shirts, pants, even underwear. I didn't understand the whole ironing thing then, and I was nonplussed as an adult, facing down another little old lady seemingly obsessed with ironing. The generation gap was as glaringly obvious as the sequins on her terrycloth visor.

"Come on," the sprightly dame enthused, as she jumped up and grabbed my hand. "I'll show you. And I'll let you have it for only a hundred bucks; it's a steal!" We walked around to a shed. Just inside was a big white metal cube on legs. She opened a front metal flap and folded up a top piece. She explained how to feed cloth into the roller. It was quite the heavy piece of machinery, this "'mangle iron." Where would I even fit it in my laundry room?

During the demonstration, she chattered on about how she had worked for So-and-so's resort; how they'd spent days washing rugs and linens in their wringer washer, hauling laundry baskets in and out to the clotheslines.

"I can relate to the wringer washer," I said. "At the resort my husband and I worked before we were married, they had a wringer. I took the sheets into town to clean at the Laundromat, but did all the heavy rugs in the wringer. Every time I talked about using it in my grandparent's presence back home in Iowa, Grampa would tease, 'Just don't get your tit caught in the wringer!' And then he'd cackle madly." I rolled my eyes.

The "mangler" maven laughed and said her husband used to say the same thing. We bemoaned the fact that accidental breast compression must have happened often, or the phrase wouldn't have been so common. I queried her about the "mangler" roller—it looked as insidiously vicious as a wringer. "Oh, yes, you need to be careful when you're threading the folds through here, too. Try not to lean in."

As we continued to exchange resort stories, my brain finally processed through reasons why I might not be in health department violation. (Besides the fact it had never been mentioned in annual inspections as of yet.) Sheets washed in hot water and tumbled in heated dryers burn off any germs or bacteria nowadays. Forty years ago, at any typical Mom & Pop Minnesota resort, air drying clotheslines and cold-water hand or wringer washers were the only items with which some folks had to work. A hot-iron press was perhaps the only regulation authorities could enforce to ensure hospitality sheets were disinfected between guests. (I have since learned that there was, indeed, a health code requiring hot-iron pressed linens which seemed to be in effect until the '70s sometime.)

I declined the enthusiastic offer of owning a "mangler." I walked away with a better appreciation for automatic washers and dryers, grateful for the luxurious modern savings of time and energy. Mostly, I walked away with mammary glands heaving sighs of relief that I had finally stopped talking about wringing and mangling.

Laura Weinberg

Poetry

At the Lake: Old Books

Botanical books
gather dust between seasons
then join our spring walks.

Matt Gregersen

Poetry

Good Earth

A chicken coop and old hog pen
Machinery never to move again
Hay rake, baler, thresher, plow
Sink into seas of grass

A wooden barn now empty
Used for half a century
Countless winters of heavy snow
Bring it crumbling down

Muscled arms and iron will
Passions that run deeper still
Blazing fires in the heart
Fade to dying embers

A lifetime is not long enough
To learn these truths that carry us
Back to the good earth
Where we all must go

Katie Gilbertson

Fiction

The Papers of Bunny Lutsky

My English teacher, Mr. Willman, loves my "unique literary perspective." I'm gathering all my writings for publication.

Gone With the Wind starts by saying Scarlett O'Hara wasn't beautiful. Who wants to read about an ugly girl, but later on she's called pretty? She sure knew how to handle guys. I picked up some pointers.

She's talking to twin brothers who won't shut up about how excited they are to go to war and beat up some Yankees. That's what people in the South called people in the North who didn't want them to own slaves. Scarlett is not a civil rights activist.

Scarlett is sulking because they're not talking about her. She goes off mad. To bring her back, they tell her that the next day, it will be announced at a barbecue that her neighbor Ashley is marrying this girl named Melanie. Scarlett has the hots for Ashley so she has a spaz attack. Scarlett is sixteen and Ashley is twenty-five. If that isn't gross enough, Melanie and Ashley are cousins. Scarlett is so stuck on herself, she decides she will tell Ashley she loves him. When he knows this, he'll dump Melanie and propose to Scarlett.

The next morning Scarlett selects a cute outfit. She is bummed she can't show her legs because they're awesome. She decides to show off the other end and wears a low-cut dress, so Ashley will notice she is prettier than ugly Melanie.

At the barbecue Scarlett gets Ashley alone and blurts out that she loves him. When he won't dump Melanie, Scarlett throws a hissy fit, but there is an eavesdropper—a man of thirty-five named Rhett Butler. Rhett is a hound and everybody knows it. He starts eyeing Scarlett 'cause she's feisty (and sixteen).

So the fun winds down because it looks like the War has started. In the excitement, Melanie's nerdy brother Charles proposes to Scarlett.

Since Ashley is lost, she might as well. Charles is rich and his parents are dead. Scarlett marries the dude, and he goes to war but dies right away from measles, leaving her pregnant, which is not in the movie.

After she has the kid, she is so bored she goes to Atlanta to stay with Melanie. She might see Ashley, home on leave. Everyone in Atlanta cares for baby Wade. She can pretend he doesn't exist. Like in the movie, where he *doesn't* exist.

Atlanta is dull. She's in mourning, wears black and can't flirt. She's mad the frumpy girls get to wear color and date army men.

The town is having a fundraiser. Scarlett can't go. She's in mourning for what's-his-name. She wants to dance. She gets a break when Melanie says she'll go with her for "The Cause." They go only to "help."

At the fundraiser, Rhett Butler bids a lot of money to dance with her—a widow! When she accepts, Atlanta is scandalized and Scarlett and Rhett dance to some screechy fiddles. After that, Scarlett does what she wants and dances her way through the war, "Supporting the Troops."

The war gets worse. Scarlett works at the hospital. The men are smelly and not interested in her. She whines because there's no parties. Plus, Melanie got herself pregnant when Ashley was home on leave. Scarlett feels like Ashley cheated on her and takes it out on Melanie, being really nasty.

Melanie is almost due and the Yankees march on Atlanta. Scarlett wants to run out on Melanie, leaving her there to die, but she figures delicate Melanie will die in childbirth anyway. She can be a heroine to Ashley by staying.

Selfish Melanie picks the day the Yankees arrive to give birth. Rhett shows up bringing a buggy to get her out. After practically killing Melanie delivering the baby, Scarlett stuffs her, the new baby, and Wade into the wagon and takes off.

It's a heinous trip. She drives the wagon over bodies. She hopes they're dead but doesn't much care. Home, she finds her sisters sick, her mother dead, and her father nuts. A few slaves are left. When Scarlett sees them in her gutted, trashed house, she orders a mint julep. She goes out looking for food and eats it out of the ground. It makes her sick and she lies on the ground puking up a radish and vows to never be hungry again. That's the end of Part One.

Marilyn Groenke

Poetry

You Don't Say

My husband took a class
"Improve Your Communication Skills."
When he came home
He didn't want to talk about it.

Deborah Rasmussen

Poetry

Suspose *(Not a Typo)*

I believed the word was real
because my grandfather always said it.

I thought it some Danish variant
a dumpling afloat in the new world
soup he ate once off the boat
missing the old country
doing his best in the new

by raising poultry and kids in Illinois
futures envisioned for both—
chickens to nourish the children
he'd vowed to educate
into better lives than farming.

Two teachers and a lawyer
were the harvest of his handiwork
all of whom forgot
the language of their father's heart
but spoke good English
and made him proud
I suspose.

Audrey Kletscher Helbling

Honorable Mention Creative Nonfiction

Josephine Holding Deloris

A hint of a smile graces her face as she looks at the camera, baby angled against her body, arms supporting the weight of her sleeping daughter.

I pull out the magnifying glass for a closer look at the details in this black-and-white photo measuring only 1 ½ inches square. I recognize the woman as my maternal grandmother, who died months after my birth. But, if not for the words—*Josephine holding Deloris*—penciled in cursive across the back of the photo, I could only guess at the baby's identity. She is my aunt, dressed on this day, likely her baptismal day, in all white with ribbons dangling from her booties.

Grandma Josephine, whom I resemble, wears a dark, short-sleeve floral dress, three strands of pearls draping her neck. The two are off-center, house behind, cement steps and a potted plant to their left. I look closer at baby Deloris, notice her full face and dark strands of hair falling across her forehead. She is every bit the picture of contentment. And Grandma, well, she appears equally as content.

The photo contrasts sharply to images I found earlier of Deloris lying in a white coffin set into a corner of my grandparents' house. I can't bear to think of that baby girl dead of whooping cough at the age of nine months and nine days on May 10, 1935.

Some ten years ago, I searched for Deloris' tombstone among the gravestones of ancestors in a rural southern Minnesota church cemetery. When I found her grave marker flush to the ground, a sadness swept over me at the loss of my grandparents' second daughter. On a simple rectangular stone slab, I read these words: DELORIS DAUGHTER OF MR. & MRS. L.L. BODE 1934-1935. I paused, considered the depth of their loss and grieved for the aunt I'd lost. And then I knelt and pulled back grass creeping onto the stone. I wanted her name fully seen. Deloris—this once sweet baby cradled in her mother's arms—deserved such respect.

I feel a strong connection to the grandmother and aunt I never knew. In July of 2005 at the age of forty-eight, I contracted whooping cough, which seventy years earlier claimed baby Deloris' life. I recovered after three months with rest and antibiotics. Unlike my aunt. At the age of forty-eight, Grandma Josephine died of unknown heart issues, which today likely could also be treated.

While I hold no memories of this mother and daughter, I have that single tiny image of the two pulled from my mom's massive photo collection. I could easily have overlooked the print as just another family photo. But its size gave me pause, drew me to look more closely. Life is like that. Sometimes we fail to see the small moments of everyday life as the moments that mean the most, that bring us the greatest joy. In the photo of *Josephine holding Deloris*, I experience joy in a mother's love spanning and connecting generations.

Jeanne Emrich

Poetry

State Fair Romance

No sooner had we passed
through the gates than we emptied
our jeans for all the romance
we could buy at concession stands.
Walking away with bleak half-smiles,
we faced a long day of penniless visits
to every free blue-ribboned hall and barn.
The August moon rose, a pitiless rock.
Lights from the midway hurt our eyes.
Carnival music blared empty promises.
We consoled ourselves by holding hands,
exhausted by our hapless silences.
We were young. We were in love.
We were broke.

Anne Stewart

Poetry

Twin Flowers

Each spring I wait for them to bloom:
the delicate twin flowers (*Linnaea borealis*)
named after the botanist who devised
the taxonomy of plants.

Paired together like new lovers,
pink blush against their bed of moss,
they clasp a miniature vine
anchored to the moment.

By mid-summer they are gone,
like the children grown, like you,
and I am left with the taxonomy
of our lives.

Victoria Lynn Smith

Creative Nonfiction

The Secret Lives of Children Sponsored by the Myth of Parental Control

When I was a child, matchbooks littered our junk drawer, loitered in gloveboxes, and stowed away under the cellophane wrapped around cigarette packs. My parents smoked; their friends smoked. Businesses gave away matchbooks with advertising logos. Butane lighters were still over the horizon, and reusable lighters required maintenance. So, matchbooks hung around my childhood.

"Don't ever play with matches," commanded my parents. Shaking our heads, my sisters and I returned wide-eyed looks clearly sending our unspoken response: *We'd never do such a thing.*

But we did.

We lit matches and held them between our fingers over an ashtray. We watched the white-hot flames flicker into molten-gold fury. When the flames neared our fingers, we dropped the matches in the ashtray. A very controlled burn.

Eventually, our experiments with fire progressed.

On the west side of our property was a large thicket of scrawny tree-like bushes. They grew to about six feet. In the summer they were covered with thick, green leaves. We'd worn narrow paths through the thicket where we played—hidden from the watchful eyes of adults.

One summer day, the neighbors, my sisters, and I entered the thicket and morphed into explorers lost in an endless, dark forest. We used all our survival skills to fend off starvation and attacks from wolves and bears. We needed a campfire to cook food and repel predators, so on our trek into the thicket, we carried an empty coffee can and several books of matches.

We gathered twigs and tufts of dried grass and stuffed them in the coffee can. The neighbor boy, having just finished sixth grade, was the oldest and in charge of the fire. He tried to light the twigs and grass, but never managed more than a few small flames, which quickly smoldered and died. Bored, we gave up and smuggled the matches back into the house at the end of the day. Over the summer, we made more attempts to build a campfire in a coffee can but had no success. We abandoned our *explorers-lost-in-the-woods* fantasy.

Our parents never discovered the game.

Forty-five years passed.

Seated at my mother's dining room table with her friends, our conversation turned to guns. Recently, a handful of accidental shootings had made the news. Children playing with unsecured handguns had caused senseless but preventable tragedies.

"Kids today don't know how to listen," my mother said. She looked at her dinner guests and continued, "When my kids were young, their dad had a handgun on the top shelf of the kitchen cupboard, and none of our kids ever touched it. They were told not to touch it, and they listened." She turned to me and asked for confirmation. "Isn't that right?"

I bristled at her smugness.

"No," I said. "We took that gun down several times and showed it to neighborhood kids."

My mother, mouth ajar, eyes wide, blanched.

I decided not to tell her about the matches and our days spent as explorers.

Jennifer Jesseph

Fiction

Crazy 8s

I am nine, the oldest; Kenny is six and Maddie is four. We are in my room playing Crazy 8s. I am teaching Kenny and Maddie to play this card game. "A diamond can go on a diamond and a matching number can go on top, too." Maddie's hands are small, so she can't hold her cards well.

My dad and their mom are going out, and we are home with a babysitter. I hear talking in the next room.

"Do you think they'll all get along? Your Julia is such a little leader. Do you see that? She's a little teacher, that one."

Their mom wants to marry my dad.

"Watch this, Kenny. See how I can put a club, this clover shape, on top? Kenny, can you help Maddie?"

Playing cards with these little kids is hard. They show their cards all the time and don't even know it.

"Good night, kids." Dad sticks his head in the room. He's all dressed up in a black suit, white shirt, black tie, and shiny shoes. He looks like a movie star. He blows us a kiss and we blow one back.

Your mom moves softly, like a cloud. She gives us each a hug and a kiss. She smells like violets. "Don't wait up," she says as she floats out of the room.

It might be a happy, happy, funny night. It's hard to tell.

They leave and we keep the game going until Kenny gets bored and Maddie wants to play with blocks.

Late at night, when we are supposed to be sleeping, I'm watching the moon and waiting. Maddie and Kenny are sleeping. I wonder what they dream.

Finally, I hear the car pull into the driveway. Doors open and shut. They come inside mumbling. The baby sitter leaves in her car.

I sit up, listening.

"Why can't we try this, why?" Their mom is crying. I can't hear my dad, but I know what's happening. She tried to put a heart on a spade, and that's not the rules.

The game is over and I go to sleep.

Tomorrow Kenny and Maddie will leave with their mom. We'll never play Crazy 8s again.

Christine Madline Ellsworth

Poetry

Kitchen Table

Close cousins drag the family farm table and two chairs
from the perspiring inside out onto the soft July lawn
nearing moonrise, for a post-picnic talk under the stars
near a lake in Becker County, Minnesota.
One hand-carved oak leg of the table sinks under an elbow
pops up with the weight of the other's and
their spilled chardonnay makes of laughter a leavening.

Within moments the glass pitcher, topped with their icy wine,
sweats a faint water sheen and sets new dark circles, hastily hand-
                              sopped
but soon enough set in the soft old wood already scarred
with Uncle Sigge's initials the night his sister Linnea arrived in '22,
the soft depression where the weekly bread was kneaded for decades,
and the corduroyed gouges set by the Allis-Chalmers Model B engine
Grandpa Josef rebuilt during the harrowing winter of 1947.

This evening, their soft, reverent voices recount the familiar old stories
of beloved godmother Astrid or the stern, hired-hand Pal or
the babies that died of diphtheria and the still that brewed hooch in the
                              '30s
when no grain would grow.
Now, the year's news—the mass shootings, hurricanes, starving Polar
                              bears—
scares them equally and with their heads close in the dark, the two talk
                              over
the faint, ghostly rings and unclaimed tattoos on the ancient table while
                              overhead,
acorns dance on the Northern Red oaks growing slowly toward the
                              farmhouse rooftop.

Insights   95

Charmaine Pappas Donovan

Poetry

Nth Generation Toy

Invented, like the wheel, in olden times,
these hoops were juggled, rolled around with sticks
by children, jesters, clowns and even mimes
who spoke in gestures while performing tricks.
Across the country, swept a new hoop craze:
a plastic ring that swung around the waist
and mimicked hula dancers' grass-hipped sways.
Some were too old to try it; some too chaste
to swivel hips like Elvis. Backs went out,
which doctors claimed was caused by hula moves.
Within this century, hula hoopers tout
more benefits in hip-rotating grooves.
Retooled toys re-circle now and then;
what goes around can come around again.

Paisley Kauffmann

Honorable Mention Creative Nonfiction

The Legend of Doug Dagnus

My mother passed the casserole to my new boyfriend, nicknamed The FBI Guy, and made one of her frequent but random comments about Doug Dagnus. She had been engaged to Doug Dagnus during her senior year of college, but called it off for reasons she could never quite explain.

The FBI Guy was broad-shouldered and handsome with cropped blond hair. He didn't smoke, drink, or go anywhere unarmed. He stopped chewing, and asked, "Did you say Doug Dagnus?"

My mother froze, her fork hovering over her plate.

The FBI Guy furrowed his brow and swallowed. "I'm sure it's not the same Doug Dagnus."

My sisters and I exchanged a look. It's not unheard of, our mother associating with men of questionable character, including her ex-husband, our father.

Holding my mother's gaze, The FBI Guy, in his measured way, said, "Doug Dagnus was the most prolific serial killer in US history. He's in federal prison serving several life sentences in Marion, Illinois."

"She went to college in Illinois," I blurted.

"What?" My mother dropped her fork. "I almost married a murderer?"

"Did you, like, kind of know?" my sister asked. "Is that why you called off the engagement? Was there something creepy about him?"

My mother shrugged and shook her head.

"That's crazy," I said. My sisters and I had our own regrets about her breakup with Doug Dagnus. Unfortunately, we would've been known as The Dagnus Girls, but maybe he was the kind of dad that cheered at softball games and helped with homework.

"Unbelievable!" My mother sat back in her chair. "He was such a polite young man."

"That's the sick thing about psychopaths," The FBI Guy said, and returned to his dinner.

Doug Dagnus became legendary. Unwittingly, our father benefited from this shocking new information, because now, relatively speaking, he wasn't so bad. He was overall indifferent towards his three daughters, and, at times, misogynistic, but he never hacked anyone into little pieces.

A year later, The FBI Guy, now my husband, refilled wine glasses as my family gathered around our star-topped tree. Cousins visiting from the East Coast had never heard about my mother's brief engagement to Doug Dagnus, the homicidal maniac. Speculating, we were eager to horrify them with vivid and gory details over smoked oysters. My husband, returning from the kitchen, laughed and said, "You believed me?"

"What do you mean?" I asked.

"I was joking."

"Seriously?" I threw a pillow at him.

"Oh no," my mother said, covering her mouth. "I called classmates from college and told them Doug Dagnus was a serial killer."

After a period of astonished silence, I said, "Maybe it's just me, but Dad seems like a total jerk again."

"Yeah." My sister sighed. "Total."

His legacy endures in our imaginations as the unsuspecting Doug Dagnus attends his college reunion. Maybe a neurosurgeon or astronaut, we picture him escorting his beautiful wife into a ballroom filled with fellow alumni mingling about and his bewilderment as the reunion dissolves into pandemonium.

Ryan M. Neely

Poetry

A Letter Home

One day
you will squint
through millennia
and recall
this putrid abyss
where you cast aside
my squandered heart.

In the moment
before regret dawns
and fractures
your ataraxic armor,
you will find me,
shining and brilliant,
winking back.

Mary Schmidt

Poetry

Grieving a Child that Never Died

Why is the day
so incomplete
still hear your voice
feel your heartbeat.

Teach me how
to leave this place
alone every day
the night, the same.

Why is the night
so full of despair
why the small hours
so hard to bear?

Teach me how
to let sorrow breathe
to love the silence
to let you leave.

Christine Marcotte

Fiction

From the Fry Pan into the Fire

Old Doc Hanson pointed to one of the men standing in the kitchen. "He's the coroner, come to see what killed your Daddy," he said.

I knew what killed him.

I did.

Doc had already told me that even though I hit Daddy with the fry pan, it might not be what caused his death. I wasn't so sure.

Before she died, Mama told me she had told Doc about Daddy. I wiped my sweaty hand on my apron and wished I could disappear. A couple more important-looking people came in. And a few neighbors. Doc said some were there to ask questions, and others to answer them.

The sheriff told me in a few minutes I would need to tell why I hit my father. I didn't know what I would say. The kitchen was hot and crowded, but still another lady sat down. Doc whispered that she would take notes. I was so scared. Daddy was still upstairs on my bed where he fell. They wouldn't let me go in, but I saw from the doorway. I wished I'd gotten him fixed up a bit better.

The sheriff stood. "It's 9:30 a.m. Sunday, September 13, 1898. I'm Sheriff Stevenson. This is the inquest of John Fredricks. At seven o'clock this morning I was summoned to the house of the deceased by Mr. Thomas Raymond, a neighbor. Elizabeth Harris has stayed with the Raymonds since 6:30 a.m. when she notified them of her stepfather's death."

The coroner cleared his throat. "Fredricks was on the bed. He was dressed in long underwear and covered. I found one wound at the back of the head where blood had clotted. I saw blood on the pillowcase, bedclothes and wall. At the conclusion of this inquest I will determine if an autopsy is required."

Another man spoke. "I'm Richard Stout, the county attorney. I have the responsibility of listening to the coroner's jury and to decide if charges will be filed. It's my understanding that Fredricks and his stepdaughter were the only ones in the house in the last twenty-four hours. We need to know what happened during that time and listen to any other evidence."

The sheriff turned to the notetaker. "Elizabeth Harris stated she struck her stepfather with a fry pan at about eleven o'clock last night. Mr. Stout will ask relevant questions of those assembled here beginning with her."

"Please explain what happened from the time your stepfather came home from work."

I gulped. All eyes were on me. I touched the thin gold ring from Mama and decided to keep my eyes on Mrs. Raymond's kind face. "Daddy came home from the mill the same time as usual, not long after five. He ate, fed animals and said he was going out."

"Where was he headed?" asked the attorney.

I shrugged. "The place he goes most since Mama died is Jones' poolroom."

"We'll need to check that," he said to the sheriff. He looked back at me. "Miss Harris, what did you do then?"

No one ever called me Miss Harris, and it took a minute to realize his question was directed at me. "I did dishes, my schoolwork, and went to visit Mrs. Raymond. I was home before dark."

"Did you light a lamp?"

"I left one set low here on the table like Daddy wants. And I went to bed."

The sheriff asked, "Didn't you tell me you brought the fry pan into your room?"

I nodded.

"You need to answer with words," he said.

"Yes."

"Why did you have it in your room?" Mr. Stout asked.

"Because Daddy's been pestering me," I whispered.

"Miss Harris," he said, "you need to explain exactly what you mean by pestering."

I twisted my hands in my apron. My face was hot, and I wished I could run from the room. Doc placed his hand on my arm and gave a slight nod of his head.

"Since Mama passed," I said, "Daddy's been grabbing me. At my bosom and my backside. Two nights ago, he came in my room while I slept. Before I could do anything, he had his pants down and was on top of me. He, —he," I stammered and buried my face into the apron.

"Does Beth need to explain anything more about that night?" Doc asked.

The county attorney looked to the sheriff. "Not now anyway. Is that the reason you had the pan? To protect yourself?"

"Yes," I said.

Lucy Tyrrell

Poetry

Blueing

In shallow cups
where the ski pole pushed,
blue light glows—
soft indigo
in the whiteness.
As blue as glacial ice,
refracted light
pockets a patch of sky.

Sue Bruns

Honorable Mention and Co-Editor's Choice Poetry

Shattered

The cup slips from my hand as I reach
for the cupboard shelf.
It nicks
the cupboard frame, springs
from my hand, somersaults
to the floor
in   slow   motion
while I, equally slowly, process what is happening.
Then, the crash—
a ceramic EXPLOSION.
HeLtEr SkELtEr—pieces skitter across the tile floor.

Then silence.

I assess the damage, step carefully, and start
to pick up the pieces—
a few large fragments,
a chipped bit of rim,
the jagged remnant of a handle.
Too much damage to repair.
I sweep up smaller scraps and flakes,
poke the broom into corners to
coax out slivers, almost invisible.

More stray pieces appear—
Sometimes a large one
I can't believe I missed
before. Days later, I'll find another shard.
Weeks later one surfaces from some narrow crevice
or the recess beneath the refrigerator or stove.

Like a shattered relationship, pieces
disperse haphazardly. Then fragments
of memories of you resurface
when I thought all had been neatly swept away.

Cindy Fox

Poetry

Anger

Heat brewed inside me
rising to a simmer
rolling into a boil
splashing hot
lashing out
stinging you

My tongue burns a sore
reminder—Why didn't I
turn off the flame
and cool down before
I scorched the pot that
will never be the same?

Always burning
always sticking
always remembering
words best unspoken
in the heat of anger.

451-8839

From the high school office in town,
I dialed those digits to call home to the farm
From my dorm at the U,
I rang only for emergencies
From my first out-of-state teaching job,
Mom and Dad cherished all calls, even collect.
To hell with the cost; we were family
We needed to hear the voices we loved

After Dad passed away,
Mom took 451-8839 to a new home in town
She kept it still at assisted living
All was well when Mom answered our ring
Then she fell, went to rehab, finally skilled care
451-8839 was not available, though my sister tried
We had dialed that number for seven decades
Now it was gone, along with our mother

Cheyenne Marco

Honorable Mention Creative Nonfiction

A Prairie Girl Sees the Ocean

The Plains have been called a lot of things. A sea. A desert. Flyover country. A dozen or so names flung at a canvas of sky and grass, meant to rein in the wild and jagged edges of prairie.

It's called so many things, but I call it "home." Born to a southwest Minnesota farm, I melted into the landscape, thrilled at the tempestuous weather, and found solace in the rhythm of corn rows. My love came on the wings of mallards and rooted with the shivering bluestem.

But for all my adult life, I've been at war, constantly defending this place as my choice. To love the Plains is to fight against the accusations of exile. Faraway voices jumping quick to criticism. *Do you ride a buffalo to school? How many feathers in a headdress? There's no one there. There's nothing there. No reason to stay.* So many souls, with darting eyes and subtle suggestions of coasts, have implied no sane person would live here. Two professors, brash and broken, told me plainly: "get out." They grumbled, their words slashing at the roots wound around my heart. Abandon the land and search for the end of the eternal sky. Try Vegas or LA or Vermont. Anywhere but here. Anywhere but home.

My defenses were met with eyerolls and murmurs of naivety. Once, I was told to see a mountain and visit the ocean. Surely, the majesty would steal me away. Surely, I would bury myself in the folds of waves or hide away in the highland.

How disappointed they must have been when I returned from Utah and Florida—not swayed by the Atlantic or taken by the Wasatch. I won't deny their majesty. My husband, quoting *The Onion*, always jokes that man is not God's greatest creation—mountains are. Personally, I find more splendor in the ocean. Maybe it's an ingrained loyalty to water, the Land of 10,000 Lakes following me wherever I go.

Still, as I stood on the boundary between earth and sea, I felt something counterfeit in the vastness. The blue-gray-green stretched beyond what I could feel. I knew, on the other side, there was a piece of land somewhere. An end to the abyss. But it was a fairy tale. Too much lay in between. It was certainly a beautiful in-between, and I would gladly fling myself into it, give myself to the fin whales and sea nettles, swim in the infinite blue. But it would never accept me as I am. It would spit me out—puckered and gasping for breath.

The Plains are a sea I can swim, a gift from the ocean haunted by the spirit of water. It has its own unending splendor: stretching and rolling and plunging. Wind stirs grasses and grains into waves. I understand why so many Plains writers compare it to the sea. I can see the ocean in it, but above all, I can feel it. It has a tide—tugging and flowing, pulling me home.

Yvonne Pearson

Poetry

Log Cabin

At dusk the cabin's fire warms us as
coyotes howl, phonics of the wild,
the pack singing to the whitened night.

The full moon washes our log walls,
trees that gave their back to my husband's adze,
their white flesh glistening with sap like sweat

in the summer sun, balanced one on another,
pinned with eighty-penny nails, walls that have
curbed and contained our wanderlust.

Inside these walls we have lain
three dolls, asleep in a row in the loft.
Only we are not playing at this.

They are breakable, these young ones.
Their breaths play a symphony of syncopation,
each marking a beat that says *I live*.

Lina Belar

Poetry

Vegetarians

We had one, once, says the dietary aide, her eyes wide with wonder as though we are some sort of exotic species. *Don't worry,* I say, *just let me see what you have to offer.* But it's not that easy. The sheet she hands me is not a real menu, but a calendar like the one they send home during the school year where the weekly selection is mac and cheese for vegetarians, a somewhat larger selection for everyone else. Fifty years removed from institutional food, it's hard to remember how that shaped our lives, an event both anticipated and dreaded, satisfying the pangs of hunger and sociability but disappointing in every other way.

Best Seller

She could see it on her phone screen with her eyes closed—*The New York Times Weekly Book Report*. The grandkids called it digital news. She subscribed with the dollar-a-month special offer.

New York Times Bestsellers
Print and E Books Fiction
22 WEEKS ON THE LIST
The Secret Life of Mignon Eberhart
An instant best seller, this fascinating debut novel by eighty-year-old Victoria Rahn centers on the life of a mystery-romance writer and her gay husband. Rahn has successfully spanned the decades from the roaring twenties to WWII, capturing the essence of the times while getting inside the heart and mind of her main character.

Her phone rang.

"Victoria Rahn." She preserved her office facade. A woman needed identity.

"Laurie Hertzel from the *Minneapolis Tribune*. Congratulations on your novel. I would like to interview you for next week's book section."

"Martin, Martin," she yelled. He was sitting right there, listening to Nora O'Donnell on CBS news, but his sister could probably hear it in California. "It's Laurie Hertzel from the *Trib*."

"Who? Who the hell is Laurie Hertzel?"

"The book editor. The *Trib* book editor. She wants to interview me. Turn the volume down!"

Her bladder held firm, thank heavens, but she needed calm. She put her phone down on the kitchen counter, grabbed the cabernet with one hand, and reached for a wine glass on the cupboard shelf with the other.

"Yes, yes, go ahead," she shouted at the phone.

"Victoria. May I call you Victoria? What inspired you to write a novel?"

"You mean at my age? Well, I'd tried poetry, memoir, nonfiction. A woman has to reinvent herself about every ten years. My ten was up."

"You've covered quite a time period. Did you remember events, or did you do extensive research?"

"Remember? I'm not that old. A year of research. Filled five notebooks."

"Do you set the research aside when you write?"

"No, I do not. I do it all at the same time. The common wisdom, and I know all the common wisdoms of writing because I've been taking classes and workshops for decades . . . decades. I could teach those classes. The common wisdom is to just write and leave blanks. Go back later. That doesn't work. And then there are the new punctuation guidelines . . . omitting commas. The Oxford comma, for Pete's sake."

"Yes, but . . . back to your research."

"If I have a question in the middle of writing a scene, scenes are critical, you have to move the story forward with scenes you know . . . I Google. Like I couldn't remember what opera is performed on New Year's Eve. My recall is pathetic these days. Oh yes, the opera. *Fledermaus.* I found a U-Tube link. Isn't U-tube incredible? I listened to the entire opera. Of course, that expended my creative energy for the day."

"I got that. Your contemporary, Faith Sullivan, uses only print sources. She has a personal library of hundreds of encyclopedias and resources. Do you use those?"

"No. NO. Faith is two years older than I am, you know. I can find anything I need with Google."

"Let's leave that. Do you have a special place to write?"

This is the big time. Interviewers always ask important writers about their writing place. Garrison Keillor's book-lined study. Sheila O'Connor's tree house. I'm prepared. I've fantasized about this forever.

"In the summer—in my loft surrounded by a clutter of blue and red notebooks, a photo of Mignon Eberhart for inspiration, her novels in an open vintage Samsonite suitcase, the spines marked with date of publication. In the winter, I write at a beach." *Not getting any younger, this is the time to come out of the closet about the beach.* "A naturist's beach."

"Really? Are you a naturist?"

"The naturists are mostly pot-bellied doctors, lawyers, merchants —emperors have no clothes—gathering at the shore as casual as at a board meeting. They raise binoculars to their eyes now and then. Scan the ocean for whales . . . and for lithe, young women strolling by."

"But are *you* a naturist?"

"I didn't say *I* was a naturist. We women sit in the shade, hatted, in full-bodied Land's End suits. Don't care to add more dermatologist's zaps and biopsy scars to our flab and wrinkles.

"I walk the beach, watch the waves— search for metaphors."

"Vickie, Vickie, wake up. You slept through CBS news again. For God's sake. And through PBS. You wanted to hear what Judy Woodruff had to say about the impeachment."

Elizabeth Weir

Poetry

When Our World Was Whole

At Sherburne National Wildlife Refuge

We near the refuge as skeins of moonlit mist lift
and we hear the music of a thousand cranes
roosting in the shallows of restored wetlands.
Behind us, the sun crowns the horizon, feathering
needles of white on frost-rimed reeds and grasses.

No wind, just the constant calling, as though
from distant beginnings in an Eocene dawn,
when creatures lived in common symmetry,
long before our coming. In a growing chorus
of wild voices, cranes rise on slow wings—
                                        ancient grace in motion.

H. A. Brown

Honorable Mention Fiction

The Astrophysicist's Wife

It started with a droplet. Transparent. Glistening. Without cruel intention. It landed, innocently enough, on a steel stud welded to the top plate of one of the many girders of a bridge under construction. The raindrop meandered down the metal pin and was blown to the edge of the flange by a gentle yet frigid wind. It reached the precipice at the exact moment its internal temperature harmonized with the chilled steel. There it stopped and rearranged its molecules into a lattice. Then it invited others to do the same. Together they formed a stalactite of ice —clear, beautiful, and heavy as it hung over a quiet stretch of Interstate 90.

It was Carl Sagan who taught me to visualize the origins of things. For thirteen amazing Sunday nights in 1980, I sat on the couch between my parents watching *Cosmos*. Carl Sagan, "everyman's astrophysicist," presented a mesmerizing depiction of how the universe came to be and how we fit in it. How small we are, the tiniest of microscopic specks really, in the scheme of the universe. And we occupy just a fraction of a fraction of a second on the calendar of the cosmos. After watching those episodes, I decided to become an astrophysicist. I wanted answers to the Big Questions. After all, there's a logical explanation for everything if you are willing to look.

I can see even farther back in time. Evidence my tiny sphere of water. Back at the beginning of everything, the molecules in my droplet were atoms that joined merrily, two hydrogens and one oxygen at a time, in the belly of a sun. As Dr. Sagan would say, "star stuff." The water molecules slammed into an infant Earth inside a parade of icy comets. A million times over they were consumed and excreted, evaporated and condensed, melted and solidified. But, on the bridge that day they were temporarily immobile, resting between gigs.

Now watch the chalkboard as I explain what happened next. First, I'll use this white chalk to represent a semi-truck carrying goods for a large grocery store chain traveling south on I-90, rumbling by at a frequency that encourages the frozen drop to vibrate. Here is a car drawn in gray, traveling north at a velocity of 72 mph on its way from Chicago to Minneapolis. See my frozen droplet represented by the red chalk? In its excited state, it decides to release its grasp on the girder flange and convinces its friends to do the same. I'll emphasize this with a thick arrow pointing down. See as they announce themselves the solution to a dynamics equation and strike the windshield of the passing car?

My wife, the solution to my personal dynamics equation, was behind the wheel of that car.

In the Spring, I took her ashes to the Superstition Wilderness and scattered the star stuff that was her across the Arizona desert. I chose the spot where we gazed in awe at the Hyakutake Comet in '96 and Hale-Bopp in '97. I unrolled our wool blanket onto the hard desert soil, took the remaining ashes in my fist and, like a Navaho sand painter, I carefully created an outline of her. Then I lay down, my hand over hers, and stared out into the cosmos.

In the beginning, was it just a drop that took her away? Or dancing molecules of frozen water that decided to let go? *(Throw your hands in the air like you just don't care?)* Or wait, was it a comet? Or the oxygen and hydrogen atoms? Without cruel intention, right? Is that right?

Sue Bruns

Poetry

Aurora Borealis

October night by the lake, we sit
in frost-laced air.
Small waves lap the shore between spaces of silence.
Your arm pulls me closer and the night air
is not so cold.
"Look!" I say and point to the light show just above the horizon
—dancing light sabers,
rippling prisms—glowing, iridescent.
Colors drown the silence
and sing in vibrant tones.
Lights—a tremolo—
reach across the sky, waver, and
weave a fluorescent latticework.
Solar winds have kicked up indigos, ionized limes,
excited bands of vibrating colors.
Light beams gyrate, wrap the night in magic.
The colors embrace us, include us, make us one with this phenomenon.
We are caught in this quivering display, this melodious whirlwind,
this shining spectacle.

Charged particles
dance above us. Electrons, protons,
and their optical emissions pull us together
with their magnetic force.

Sharon Harris

Poetry

A Moment Dancing

smoke was thick, alcohol flowed like water in spring
tables were filled with girls
       and guys who watched them
rock music filled me like another heartbeat
I could hardly sit still
       in the pulsing room

recently divorced and fresh from a breakup
I was lonely though surrounded by friends
here I was, starting over again
not a good place to be
I cautioned myself
       to guard my newly damaged heart

then there was a touch on my shoulder
a stranger had come
       to ask me to dance
I could tell with one glance
oh yes, here was trouble
in the shape of a man
my favorite looks, long dark hair
       trim beard and moustache
a flash of white teeth
danger in his sparking blue eyes

so different from the others who were there
tall laced-up boots, a coat with a red plaid hood
       spread out over broad shoulders
he took my hand
and led me to the dance floor
       put his arm around me
       like it was his right
and just like that
stole away my careful heart

Adam McFarlane

Fiction

Secret Santa

On December weekends, I work at Valhalla, a 500-square-foot booze house between Brainerd and Mille Lacs. It's little more than a dilapidated shed with tables and chairs. But it feels like home.

At the end of the bar, a woman ordered a White Christmas (think a White Russian with horchata and cold press). Her luxuriantly thick, mahogany mane flowed smoothly behind her shoulders. Unfazed by the cold, dry air—was it combed with dryer sheets? A strand playfully curled in the way of her brown eyes, Veronica Lake-style. She was too old for college, too young for marriage.

"Looking for someone?" I asked.

She handed me an invitation. "He said he'd be here."

It was a greeting card embossed with metallic blue snowflakes on a steel pink background. *Liz. Want to meet? Dec. 16 @ Valhalla. 3 pm. From: Secret Santa.*

"You're Liz?"

Nodding, she said, "It came with a box of chocolate-covered pecan clusters."

"Your Secret Santa is a secret admirer?"

She nodded again.

After turning off the space heater, I stepped away to change the stout tap. When I returned, a man sat next to her. He ordered a Guinness. His black polo and fleece pullover went with his sienna hair and matching eyes.

"I know you from somewhere, don't I?" she asked.

Mike was a lawn-, snow-, and handyman for several resorts. He shrugged. "Do you?"

The bar wasn't long enough for stool space between Mike and other folks. And Valhalla's not the kind of place where customers had to ask, "Is someone sitting here?" Still, I suspected, she couldn't tell whether Mike sat beside her by chance or if he was her Secret Santa.

"Any kids in elementary school?" she asked.

He gave a huff of amusement. "I work for the district when the resorts are slow. But kids myself? Heck, no."

She toyed with the invitation, but put it away when he took out his phone and started scrolling with a finger.

I suggested, "Maybe your secret admirer is really shy. Maybe he's married. And he chickened out."

"Or," she said with a sigh, "it's just a big joke, and I've come here for nothing."

"You have a secret admirer?" Mike asked.

She nodded and showed him the invitation.

Mike shrugged. "Maybe he's old, and it just wouldn't work out. But he wanted to express himself anyways."

"Why would he ask me to meet him in the first place, then?"

"Good point," he admitted. "How do we know it's a guy?"

The discussion orbited around Secret Santa for a while. The room was half-full—only ten people. Mike focused on his phone, chatting, depositing his two cents. She finished her drink, then took a last glance around. "My name is Liz Wright. You can find me all over social media. If you ever want to hang out sometime, DM me. Not my classroom page, but my personal stuff."

Mike nodded and smiled.

After she left, I said, "Funny thing, that Secret Santa card. Looked like it had your handwriting."

He gulped the last ounce from his glass.

"Wouldn't it have been easier to introduce yourself in 'normal life'? Or admit to sending the card?"

As a secret admirer, you could express feelings without risking rejection. But how do you come out of hiding and still save face?

He smiled. Maybe Mike found a way. "I like this better."

Niomi Rohn Phillips

Fiction

Facebook—You Have a Message

Daniel Reish—Rosemary Hillen, I found your name on the Facebook class list for the fiftieth Bergdorf high school class reunion. Is your maiden name Weiss? Perhaps we knew each other?

Rosemary—My maiden name is Weiss. Yes, we knew each other. We knew each other well.

Daniel—Where are you located now?

Rosemary—Seattle, Washington.

Daniel—How did you end up in Seattle?

Rosemary—Dad put me on the train to Seattle the day after graduation. I lived there with my aunt for several months and never went back to Bergdorf.

Daniel—I left that summer after high school graduation too. Keith Axtman and Phil Fettig and me. We enlisted. Got out of Bergdorf to see the world. The world turned out to be Vietnam. Do you go back to North Dakota?

Rosemary—Only for my parents' funerals.

Daniel—In fifty years? Don't you have relatives in the area?

Rosemary—Yes. A large extended family.

Daniel—You don't visit them in Bergdorf?

Rosemary—Among other reasons, my husband is a Protestant, and the family never liked him. Some hurts never heal. Where do you live?

Daniel—San Francisco. I was discharged there and didn't want to go home. I didn't want to farm, and Ma expected me to take over the farm.

Rosemary—I remember your mother. And one painful visit to your farm. The meadow larks were singing like our happiness when we got out of the car. The fragrance of red and white peonies along the walk and fronting the wide porch made me smile. The hired girl met us at the door and led us from a foyer into the biggest parlor I'd ever seen. You held my hand. Yours was sweaty. You introduced me to your mother. She was very polite.

Daniel—I remember *you.* May crowning at St Michael's. You were the Queen of the May. My Queen. I sat with my dad and brothers on the right side of the church—the men's side. I'm sure you remember that tradition. Women on the left. Men on the right . . . Queen of the May with your maiden court in long, pastel dresses and crowns of flowers. You were beautiful. I was sure Ma would see and realize how impressive you were. How important. She'd come around.

Rosemary—She didn't though, did she? Just the daughter of the local scrap dealer. The man who warmed the stool in Andy's tavern nearly every night of the week. I waited those last days of school before graduation—hoping you would find me in the hallway, offer me a ride home. We could park again near those grain bins in the country. All would be well.

Daniel—I'm sorry for my cowardice.

Rosemary—I looked for you after Mass the Sunday before I left for Seattle. A prominent Catholic family like yours never missed Mass. Then I realized you had probably come into town for the 8:30 Mass to avoid me.

Daniel—I didn't know how to challenge Ma. I was only seventeen years old, Rosemary. I thought I would wait and let her cool down. But then when I asked about you around town, you were gone.

Rosemary—I was only seventeen too, but I couldn't wait to grow up . . . or for you to grow up. I had no choice in that matter.

Daniel—I remember you talked about being a journalist.

Rosemary—I had to give that dream up. What about you? Your dream?

Daniel—I took advantage of the GI Bill after Vietnam. Went to Berkley where I met my wife. She was born and raised in California.

Rosemary—Do you have children?

Daniel—No. My wife and I have had a pretty successful realty business. Do you have a family?

Rosemary—I had a son. He's fifty years old now. My husband and I have two daughters—all grown and married—eight grandchildren.

Daniel—Do you plan to come to the class reunion? I would like to see you very much. Learn more about your family.

Rosemary—No. I won't be there. I've never attended high school class reunions. Living down the past in a small town . . . the shame clings forever like fuzz on black wool. I don't need a reunion to remember our graduation year. I have a living reminder. And . . . I am too old, and it is too late to renew ancient relationships.

Patricia Kemmerick

Poetry

The Call

The lake is calm
Night draws near
The loons call
"Where are you?"
Fog is slowly setting in
Trees appear faint and distant
It is so peaceful
My heart is at rest
"I am here," I reply
"I am here."

Lina Belar

Poetry

City Sidewalks

In the boulevard between the curved walk
peopled by runners and bicyclists
parading in neon-colored spandex
and the four-lane highway where traffic
rages in obedience to precision-controlled
traffic lights lies a springy turf of grass
home to a world of miniature flowers.

No signs draw attention to their existence
but I am of an age where a morning walk
is more a quiet saunter and, like children and dogs,
I am easily distracted. Today, it's not shiny toys
or gum wrappers that catch my eye but the tiny,
unnamed, unheralded harbingers of spring.

I notice first the wild strawberries,
their daisy-like flowers towering
two inches above the rest. By summer,
they might produce fruit for the birds
if the lawnmower spares them. Closer to ground,
blue flax flowers rise above swords of grass,
stars dotting the heavens above a miniature world.

Nestled at the soil line are pea-sized yellow flowers
like the wooden balls of a miniature croquet game
abandoned when the players stopped for tea.
I imagine joining the game, treading carefully
around the sharp blades of grass while high above
a fluffy dandelion explodes, showering me with silk.

Marlys Guimaraes

Poetry

Chicken Yoga

It had to be done. The chicken coop is not self-cleaning.
Offensive ammonia smells, disgusting manure piling up
under the roost, winter threatening, and no volunteers.

It had to be done. Rubber boots to my knees, brown
work gloves, a pitchfork and screeching resistance from
ten rust-colored hens, one rooster, and two guineas.

It had to be done. I bent and stretched like downward
facing dogs to scoop under soiled straw and pick up
chunks of matted manure, then suspended my breath
until I reached the compost pile and flung.

It had to be done. A warrior's stance allowed me to reach
into corners, humming little *om*'s as thoughts of mice leaping
out from under dried straw threatened to paralyze me.

And when it was done, cobwebs removed, fresh-smelling straw
on the floor, waterers replenished, I bowed to the chickens,
thanking them for their daily egg supply.

Then I bowed to the compost pile, now a smelly mass
that will convert hay, straw, manure, garden and food waste
into dark, rich soil to feed the plants that we eat.

It was done. I was ready for Savasana's deep
relaxation pose, a shower and a Coke on ice.

Nicole Borg

Poetry

Afternoon Worship

In my own made-up religion
after confessing to sins
real and imagined
the priestess advises
Plant a garden—peas,
beans, onions green,
heirloom carrots, slim hot peppers,
Ruby Queens—and instead
of doing my penance
Hail Mary, full of grace
on the plastic rosary beads,
I must pull a spiritually significant
number of weeds. On my knees,
hands plunged in loam,
dirt deep under my nails,
I consider what I have done
and sometimes failed to do.
The little pile of warming,
wilting weeds, atonement
for sins of pride and greed
and general human curmudgeonliness.
I listen to the birds' songs
feel their church-choir voices
in my chest, breathe
the heady incense of lilacs, drink
stained-glass collage of impatiens,
snapdragons, begonias, yard decor
sparkling with otherworldly luminescence.
In my church-garden
everything, all of it, in this moment
straining toward light.

Jeanne Everhart

Creative Nonfiction

A Country Girl Living in Town

Deep drifts cover squirrel trails under a palette of white sky and grey shadows. Snow descends sideways, making travel difficult. I see beauty in winter's falling flakes and after-the-storm stillness and a new landscape. In my recliner my thoughts travel over game trails, through Minnesota woods filled with birdsongs as I search for my sense of place. My mind explores along riverbanks, and wanders knee-deep in pasture grass and wildflowers. This old body and legs are no longer physically able to walk these paths, so they journey in glimpses of memory as I drift with the snowfall.

When I lived in the country I marveled at the ever-changing lake, the colorful sunrises and sunsets, wildlife, loon calls and changing seasons. Now I live in town and thoughts cling to those rural scenes that I never tired of. Here, from my window, I survey a grassy field that slopes into cattails and is rimmed by old oak of a small woods above the golf course. I imagine this ideal wildlife habitat is my park.

Identifying birds coming to feeders and watching the pecking order makes me smile. Springtime brings splashes of color with orange Orioles and yellow plumage of Goldfinch. Squirrels race limb to limb through trees with fluffy tails unfurled. Rabbits have an afternoon schedule for nibbling grass and leafy plants. Baby bunnies are a delight hiding in my patio summer garden as I water flowers. A fox is a regular neighborhood visitor. The antics of the gorgeous red-coated fox enchant me, like the thrill of deer strolling through and giving me reason to stop everything and watch. An occasional skunk, feral cat, turtle, and even a woodchuck have come through my backyard sanctuary in town.

Living in town, I still get little glimpses of red and gold sunrises or sunsets or billowing thunderheads above rooftops and around street lights and signs. It is not quite the same as the untouched expanses at the lake, but a little reminder. I remember the full moon rising over the lake and reflecting across the water unobstructed by houses. I must search more closely now for those special moments—looking and listening for a tiny frog on a new flower blossom, or the flutter of hummingbird wings. There is delight watching a painted lady butterfly choose one of my flowers to sip nectar from.

My world is shrinking, as I become more aware of small pleasures. Youthful country trails are on the other side of my window now. I am finding my sense of place in this new landscape in town.

Ruth M. Schmidt-Baeumler

Poetry

Dinner for One

It's eaten its way through the stomach
shouldn't it be satisfied now?

But no,
the cancer cloud with the name
like a Greek warrior, Adeno,

silently slinks on, seeks
nourishment for its troops

who develop through apomixis,
need nothing but themselves
for reproduction,

slither through lymph nodes
prey on esophageal tissue.

A march of death motes
just taking care of themselves

like humans at a meal
this dinner for one host.

Mary Jones
Poetry

When Death Came

When the family gathered at her bedside,
they reminisced about her life,
discussed politics and weather and sports
and children and recipes.
But she was beyond caring.

When they left, taking with them
their noisy talk, leaving behind their empty
Starbucks cups and candy wrappers and
doughnut crumbs, she saw the events of her life
unfold before her, as though
she were a little girl again watching
autumn leaves float down
the stream behind her childhood home.
Voices and scenes from long ago, her first bike,
her first kiss, her first baby,
everything suffused with rosy light.

When Death came, it came not as a
Grim Reaper, or an Angel of Light,
but as a Compassionate Friend.
She welcomed it for she was tired
and had been ill so long.

When Death came, it came as serenely
as a winter sunrise over a frozen lake,
orange and purple and pink streaking the sky,
snow heaped high on pine branches.

When her daughter, awakened early by the
phone call, ventured out to see that sunrise,
a cardinal sang to her from the ash tree,
then flew away.

Tara Flaherty Guy

Creative Nonfiction

Ice Prayer

Skates tightly laced, I slid rubber guards over my blades, then carefully navigated the raised threshold of my kitchen door. In the frigid darkness, unsure of my footing on the frozen ground, I pinwheeled my arms for balance, then began walking with the rigid, rocking stride common only to toddlers, Frankenstein and skaters not on ice. *Cold.* Serious cold, instantly freezing the moisture in my nose and throat, frosting my eyelashes. The cold of my childhood. Skate-guards tangling in the frozen grass, I moved toward the corner of my house, head down, watching my feet.

The bare ice on the lake was new but solid, thanks to an unusually hard freeze at Thanksgiving, and I wanted to catch a handful of rare, starry nights on the ice before the snow flew; such nights were really the only kind of prayer I indulged in anymore. Breath rising in ghostly frost-plumes around my face, I rounded the corner and glanced up, drawing a quick, awed breath. Before me, the lake was a shimmering ebony mirror reflecting a huge harvest moon beginning its slow ascent over the eastern horizon. It floated above the glittering obsidian plain, half-obscured behind jagged black pines on the far shore. I stood still, breathless, thinking *I can see it rising.*

It was true. With the moon so close, so enormous, its movement was perceptible to the naked eye. As it rose it spilled pure, radiant light through the branches, over the trees, and onto the dark, gleaming lake. Like molten gold pouring from a crucible, it spilled across glimmering onyx to me on the western shore. In its thrall, I began to stumble downslope toward the rocky beach, rapt, a Luna moth drawn to an icy flame. The word *moonstruck* floated through my mind, and I thought, *I know what that means, now.*

Unscarred by skate, or ski, or sled, the lake was black silk. I launched from the shore, a night bird lifting from its branch in a quiet rush of wings. Then I was flying, flying on the luminous path, twirling in the golden light, breathing in the radiance, part of the earth, part of the heavens, part of the night. I lifted my cold face to the sky, spinning, skimming on the shining moon-path. Under new stars winking into life, I spun and twirled in the cold air scented by pine and the frost-spray from my blades, for minutes or hours or days, feeling a rapture almost holy, like a sacrament.

At last I slowed my spinning, slower, then slower, until I stopped, completely still, even my breath. Whether from my sudden stop, or the slow, graceful wheeling of the stars in the night sky, I felt dizzy, tiny, inconsequential in my smallness. The vast, frozen silence seemed ferocious, the moment sacred. Far below the sparkling indigo vault of the cathedral sky, I bowed my head in wordless prayer.

Norita Dittberner-Jax

Co-Editor's Choice Poetry

Plainsong

For Kate

My first days of chemo she brought
vivid blossoms from her garden,
the opposite of sick.

My only work those long days
to bring fresh water and cut the stems.
Being natural as rain, they did not last

but their frail beauty anchored me.
In the austerity of nausea, a bouquet of lilies,
and bush roses, not so red as cherry.

On the day radiation started,
when I put on the mask that bolted me
to the table, hydrangea. Three varieties.

My poem for Kate is plain—I know only
common names. She knows their specific names,
the sound of them like Baroque fancies.

In my time of cancer, that long summer,
I remember the treatment, yes,
and yes, armfuls of lilies with dark centers.

Enough

Beyond my bedroom window, the frenzy at hanging feeders and suet baskets predicts this sunny winter afternoon will not last. Nut-and-Berry Wild Bird Blend—always a favorite with the chickadees and nuthatches —disappears faster than I can replenish it. Woodpeckers—downy, hairy, red-bellied, pileated—queue on porch railings to take turns devouring the last block of Audubon Park Peanut Delight. Radar confirms the birds' forecast: winter weather warning—fast-approaching low bringing a blast of snow and biting wind whistling in off the Canadian Rockies. Focused on their frenetic feasting, my feathered friends scarcely notice the intrusion as I step outside to stroll across the deck. Smoothly sliding the patio door shut behind me, I gauge the shifting wind and dwindling food supply, then scrape up particles of peanuts, seeds and tallow. The pileated's non-stop pounding on what's left of the suet prompts a sobering prediction of my own: these precious morsels will have to last the birds until this Alberta Clipper blows itself out.

sunny winter day
frenzied suet feast foretells
Alberta Clipper

Dorothy Anderson

Honorable Mention Humor (Creative Nonfiction)

The Ladies Who Brunch

Our group of women from the neighborhood, most well over the age of sixty, enjoy getting together once a month for food and chat. We share information about families, health, the neighbors, commiserate, laugh and generally enjoy each other's company. Being of like ages and similar backgrounds, we have shared some rather personal events and situations in our lives, but we tend to keep it light—especially if we are eating in a restaurant rather than in a home.

This particular month, we decided to meet at a restaurant in a local casino. We have met there before as their brunch menu is good and the restaurant is isolated from the gaming floor. Table service can be slow, however; rarely is any patron in a hurry.

Before and after food service, the conversation streams ebbed and flowed around the table and eddied at particularly interesting topics. Advice and pancake syrup were freely distributed. Three ladies started a side conversation about the foxes in the area which grabbed everyone's attention, topic being: what is the name of a group of baby foxes?

Cindy and I looked it up on our phones. Google provided information on the life span, mating and pup-care of the common red fox which I shared in a loud voice so the ladies at the far end of the table could hear.

Then I shared my donation of ancient deer meat to a friend's dogs. We all jumped on the topic raft about deer hunting and went hurtling through the conversation rapids.

Fueled with caffeine, no sub-topic about deer hunting was off-limits for our group. Besides hunting tales, we all seemed to have rapid-fire opinions on Chronic Wasting Disease: where you took the deer; testing; what meat you could eat if the deer tested positive; whether you had to bring in the whole carcass or could gut it in the field and then bring the bag of guts; what one did with a bag of guts, head and spine, even the hide, from a positive deer; how long one could leave the guts in a deer before the meat started to rot, etc., in rather graphic detail.

It was no surprise when the guy from the next table held up his hand and asked us to stop talking about deer guts and dead meat as he was trying to eat his breakfast. He explained he was a hunter. He just didn't want to hear about "bag of guts" and such when he was cutting into his steak.

We all stopped talking a nanosecond, then burst out laughing and simultaneously apologized to the man who assured us that no harm had been done. He admitted to enjoying the information about the foxes so the conversations must have been rather loud. It was also the moment I realized that the surrounding tables were now empty.

Lynn then jokingly announced, "Well, at least we didn't talk about childbirth!"

A look of horror washed over the man's face.

Viola LaBounty

Poetry

Butterflies, Every One

Women I have come to know in my life
        tend to be elusive.
Creative in ways that astound me,
        interesting, captivating, strong.
Hours pass by in moments of conversation.
We laugh together until breathless.
When time comes to part,
        we linger
        at each other's door,
        on street corners.
We find threads to continue
        our connection.
Like butterflies do,
        one will drift away on her own.
I, not daring to touch delicate powder
        on wings,
        halt her flight,
prevent her glorious freedom to be alone,
        release her.
I long to know better, each, every one.
But how do you hold butterflies
        without touching their wings of freedom?
We share tender secrets,
        uphold through storms.
Words fail me.
        Each woman, irreplaceable,
offer one another encouragement
        when, may seem,
        all is gone.

Cheryl Weibye Wilke

Poetry

Sidewalk Families

I recall the sidewalks bustling
with moms and dads, grandparents,
ladies sporting handkerchiefs and
heels, the men in dungarees and work
boots. Saturday's main street sidewalks
aflutter with American flags, Memorial
Day's crepe paper poppies, and paved
or patched generations of small town
families.

Pam Whitfield

Creative Nonfiction

Winter Fashion Sense

Winter has arrived: the season when Minnesotans can give the middle finger to fashion and wear whatever feels good. Since this season lasts half the year, it is possible for women to get pregnant, carry a baby to term, have it, and then meet their neighbors during a spring stroll, only to hear, "We didn't know you were pregnant!" A stadium-length down parka can hide a lot.

I've always loved women for their practicality. Now that I live in Minnesota, I worship this quality. Up here, the women don't have time to fret about a little winter weight gain. They're too busy clearing ice dams off the roof or dragging the wet-dry shop vac down to the basement.

Every November, they start cooking stews and curing venison. They eat like the holidays are coming—because they are. These are women who know what a serious day's work feels like, and their pioneer instincts tell them to slow down for winter because spring planting will come soon enough.

I like that slowing down part: the idea that fireplaces, books, and glasses of wine are legitimate companions of an evening. I like how every outdoorsy or farm-living woman I know has *two* wardrobes. This, my friends, is not extravagance. It is thrift and sensibility. When they gain that inevitable ten or fifteen pounds, they have clothes ready and needn't shop. Ben Franklin would approve.

My farming friends refer to the Fat Closet. As in, "These are my fat pants. Boy, am I going to have to hoe a lot, come April." Inevitably, they do. The garden needs tilling, the barnyard must be shoveled out, the driveway is due for resurfacing; these women are handy with tools and tractors. The pounds slide right off their frames like wet snow off a pole shed roof on a sunny day.

Which gives them permission to go to their Skinny Closet, pick out something cute, and do the summertime equivalent of that fireplace/book/bottle of wine ritual: the backyard barbecue. While her man holds court with a spatula and a plate of brats, the Minnesota woman is steering her guests, slicing pie, making clever comments, and generally showing off in those skinny clothes. It's July, and she is her slender, freckled, sun-washed, high-spirited self again.

This is harmony with the seasons, a perfect human ingenuity—if only we will go with it, instead of fighting it.

Ladies, the next time you step on the scale and see it's given you three new pounds, do not distress. You are right in line with your ancestors. This is Mother Nature making you more cuddly for your honey under the duvet. This is evolution giving you backup fuel and padding and warmth all at once.

Wear that padding with pride! Nobody will see it under that Fleet Farm canvas coat anyway. But come April, get off your duff and start showing some pioneer quality. I'm counting on you to keep my Nordic myth alive.

Ed Brekke-Kramer

Poetry

Polished

To pick up one
stone from a stream
serendipity

a slightly less than random act

a pebble for a pocket
smoothed by stream flow
rolled along a run
by drizzled rain and summer storm
down across a reach of life
comes to rest
to wait
unwittingly

Adrian S. Potter

Poetry

Suggestions for Writing Poetry

Journals with ochre-tinged pages
can be indispensable. When considering
topics, beware of the long-winded and trite.
You never know when vices might provide
inspiration, particularly while dancing
with narrow-waisted strangers at dive bars.

Remember obscurity invents mystery.
Liquor may also help. A camisole beneath
a silk blouse may mend the awkward
interstices between line breaks.

Imagery always makes an impression.
Kudzu adorning telephone poles like stockings.
Rain-slicked streets glazed with the vulgar light
of strip clubs. Resentment smoldering
like a lit cigarette tossed onto the sidewalk.

Expect nothing. Prepare for everything.

For every trap door or frayed roadmap,
draw a red X across your forehead.
Do not censor questionable thoughts
or preach the false gospel of optimism.

On Saturdays, teach the skyline how to be
an exit wound and flirt with the uncertain
havoc of a fragmented future. Mention
crimes and failures without context and
let the reader sort through the carnage.

Resist having tidy conclusions.

Marlys Guimaraes

Fiction

Reading the Tea Leaves

Tea latte foam plays on my lips until a heat-sucked whistle tells me to slow down, pay attention. Ned's words sink my netted tea bag. I lift the orange and green tag to watch, dangle, and dare. One has to be still in order to see tiny bubbles smiling on the cup's edge. Shreds of Anahola Granola drop from my fingers like misplaced kernels of popcorn. I pick up my purse and leave him, a crumpled napkin at a dirty table.

Janice Larson Braun

Poetry

Illumination

Just as a spider web—
Nearly invisible in the grass—
Blooms radiantly
When bejeweled with morning dew,
So love
Hidden deep in the heart
Glows luminously
When adorned with tears.

Sharon Harris

Poetry

Sunday Mornings

when you were here
Sundays were my favorite mornings
we'd get up slow
cuddle a little
stretch and move as we wished
with no to-do list beckoning
no outside expectations

CBS Sunday Morning
the show we both liked
murmured in the background
while I fixed a big breakfast
eggs scrambling
sausage sizzling in the pan
honey drizzling across toast

and I picture you
in your house now
getting up slowly
stretching and moving
nothing special to do today
morning TV on as background
fixing a big breakfast
and maybe remembering
Sunday mornings
with me

Dorothy Anderson

Fiction

Talisman

She read the fading scrap of paper every day. It was held by a tourist magnet on the side of the refrigerator. She didn't remember exactly when she received it in a fortune cookie, only that it had struck a chord of hope and anticipation in her young heart at the time.

You will spend your old age surrounded by comfort and wealth.

Eleven simple words that she interpreted at thirty-one as a wish for the future, a bright, comfortable future that she worked so diligently to achieve. As she hacked her way through the corporate jungles, she always had an eye on the long game. She saved. She invested. She tried to ensure that every new job was a step up in income. She bought her first home at a time when her contemporaries spent their money on new cars and destination vacations.

Because of her laser focus on building a career, she chose marriage later in life to a man who had already stuffed his future's comfort cushion and was as adamant as she that they protect their hard-won assets. They also donated to worthy organizations each year to, hopefully, alleviate any karmic debt. They looked forward, together, to fulfilling the fortune's prophecy, to an old age surrounded by comfort and wealth.

In all the houses, on all the refrigerators, she read the fortune every day, repeating the words in her head as a mantra. "You WILL spend your old age surrounded by comfort and wealth."

Her husband's old age was cut short by the cancer diagnosed eighteen months after he retired. Neither prayer nor modern medicine could deter the disease's progression as it wore away his body and their finances. She decided to retire early.

Their financial adviser strongly advised her to divorce him so that the cost of his care would be absorbed by the State, but she refused. She knew they were, truly, "spending their old age," and accepted it as necessary for his care. Each time she had to liquidate assets to pay for his drugs and hospitalizations, she also wondered what "comfort and wealth" would be left for her in the future. When the bills and late fees grew faster than his cancer, she took a job at sixty-seven to hold off the creditors. She sold their house to pay for his hospice care and moved in with a friend until he died.

The bills didn't die when he did. She sold everything but the car and whatever keepsakes she could move into an efficiency apartment, using the proceeds for the apartment's down payment and to pay off some of the outstanding balances.

Now she smiled wryly each time she read the fortune on the apartment's refrigerator. The building was nearby a new, upscale "retirement community" where she found employment as an administrative assistant. Her manager was old enough to be her grandchild.

She couldn't afford to live there. However, she was surrounded by comfort and wealth. Perhaps the fortune's prophecy was fulfilled.

Kathryn Ganfield

Poetry

White-tailed

Three does, in day's gray light,
bed beyond the fallen timber. Laid low by the wind,
like matchsticks, cavaletti.
Tucked, clay forms
dun against the snow.

Noses black briquettes, chins dipped in snowflakes.
Ears like valleys, where forest snaps resound
and quiver in coarse hair tips.

More does at night,
so many more. Unnumbered.
They flee like dust motes before
a buck relentless.
He is all pairs: antlers, buckeyes, stones.
Harried, but still these does laze their hooves atop the snow.
A-dot, a dash,
and then—ellipses.

Sonja Kosler

Poetry

Thrift Store Shopping

rows of discards
cleaned-out clutter
treasure may lurk

an embellished wooden box
deserves space in my home
nothing else today

at the counter a flimsy paperboard container
holds a jumble of silvery spoons—
miniature souvenir spoons

memories of travel, adventure, escapade
chosen from gas station tourist shop displays
added to prized collections back home

Auntie Lillian collected thimbles.
Her sister, Gladys, favored shot glasses.
Daughter Terri adored all things bovine
until she found true love.

This thrift store space holds
memories with no one to remember.

Yet, a box of spoons reminds
of shoes and eye glasses
once gathered and discarded
at a place named Auschwitz.

Cindy Fox

Fiction

Babysitting the Grandkids

I arrive at my son's house just before three on Friday afternoon. He and his wife take turns apologizing and thanking me for babysitting over the weekend. I wave it off like babysitting is no big deal. They haven't been out since Trump was elected president. They deserve time alone. I hold three-year-old Eli's hand and walk them to the door.

"You two have a great time. Heck, stay 'til Monday if you want."

"Thanks again, Mom," my son says. "We'll be home Sunday afternoon." I try to say goodbye, but Eli is jabbering at the same time. "You kids be good for Grandma," my daughter-in-law yells over her shoulder.

The door shuts. The kids scatter like mice. They have their work cut out. There's a house to destroy, a sibling to torture, and a grandmother to disobey. Eli reappears and we stare at each other. The terrible truth dawns on him. Mommy's gone and I'm here. A rotten trade. His face puckers like he just ate a sour grape.

Ellie, *way* too grown up to be six years old, competes for my attention. Eli's sobs subside as his sister models her new princess dresses, performs gymnastics, shows me her artwork. I cringe when she opens a can of lime green slime and loops strands around her arms. She giggles when I try to grab the can. Who invents stuff like this for kids? Probably some grownup kid whose mother didn't get mad when he went to sleep with bubble gum in his mouth.

I check on Eli, who's migrated downstairs to the playroom. The room is a broken ankle waiting to happen. If it rolls, it's on the floor— footballs, baseballs, basketballs, toy tractors, skateboards. He's in the corner talking to himself when he swings at the batting tee. He yells, "And he scores!" just as a tennis ball whizzes past my ear.

Back upstairs, the kids want to watch a video they've seen forty times. They lay on their stomachs, their heads arched back, looking up at the screen three feet away, positions that would paralyze an adult. Their wide eyes drink in the blue flickering light. I make a bowl of popcorn and they scramble to the couch, one on each side of me. I'm amazed how black and white cartoons have evolved into Technicolor 3D animated movies and no longer involve a cat and mouse killing each other. *Frozen's* teachable moments about sisterly love do not escape me. If the grandkids want to watch it for the forty-first time, that's okay by me.

Bath time. Eli squeezes a plastic frog under the water and giggles when air burps on the surface. "Grandma, did you hear Kermit toot?" Hilarious. What a ham! Ellie bathes a Barbie doll which I question but she insists it's okay. Something about green slime in her hair. I lift Eli out of the tub. He streaks through the house like a fireball.

Getting Ellie to brush her teeth is not easy. She decides it is comedy night. "Grandma, I forgot how to brush my teeth." Picking up a hairbrush she says, "I can't get this in my mouth!" Her smile shows off missing teeth, the other half grade-school jagged.

Bedtime negotiations are complex and trying, much like convincing homebody Grandpa to take a winter vacation with me. Their demands are endless and unreasonable. The number and length of stories to be read. Where I have to sit when I read. The amount of light that must be let into the room before I can shut the door. I try persuasion, scolding, reverse and double-reverse psychology. Only the blessing of fatigue works.

Sunday afternoon. I've resigned to sit on the couch and do nothing. The living room floor is littered with toys. Globs of Tater Tot Hotdish are smeared on the dining room chairs. Why bother picking up after them anymore? I tried. I failed. I'm tired, too. Last night the dog began whining and whimpering at three a.m., no doubt missing its special humans. My eyes are heavy, my head bobbing down when I hear tires on the driveway.

"Oh, no sweat!" I lie. "I'd be glad to babysit again, soon, please!"

My son and his wife laugh at what a liar I am. For them tomorrow means the kids will be fed, washed and put to bed, every day for the thousands of days that it takes. Every day a miracle of patience sustained by love.

Laura Weinberg

Poetry

Morning After Windfall

The old oak still stands
and the battle-scarred pine tree leans
forward toward Spring.

Richard Fenton Sederstrom

Poetry

Some Small Thing, Tan

A tan insect
not a mosquito but tan
not so dull as the tan of the mosquito—

brighter
a little yellow in the mix perhaps.
Certainly not a mosquito

or I would be slapping
and I would have enjoyed scant guilt and scanter sorrow

in the matter because of
the customary cold wave of colder recognition:

the Mosquito—
her poisonous reputation.
But this tan with its bit of yellow, jumps

and scampers in the sun on the arm of the swing
like a hot-sand sand flea or
an electrified puppy.

We share the same sun, the same swing.
We are entertained by

the same shocks of fear and the same stunned
shocks of release.

Decide with us
while light shines on these pranks,
to share the antics of evolving.
            "Yip!"

Maurice Spangler

Honorable Mention Humor (Fiction)

Dumboy

I was nonchalantly reading a local newspaper and saw the following ad.

The Snazziest Winter Driveway in Northern Minnesota Contest.

Rules: You must have the most beautiful winter driveway as determined by judges who will inspect your driveway regularly during the contest period.

Last entry date is Dec. 15. Competition concludes Mar. 15.

Points are awarded based on the following criteria: Snow edges must be crisp and sharp. Surface must be smooth with no dirt, car debris, plant debris, or animal excrement anywhere. There must be no vehicle tracks visible. Sculptures on the sides of the driveway are encouraged with extra points awarded if they are colored, lighted, and wired for music.

Grand prize is $15 with a most prestigious certificate given.

Entry fee: $250.

Sponsored by Driveways Undergoing Midwinter Beautification, Oh Yeah! (DUMBOY).

I'm Bob from Park Rapids, Minnesota, by the way—Todd Township actually. I pay part of my property taxes to Henrietta Township where my garage is, but my house taxes go to Todd. This is beside the point, however, since this article is about driveways.

I was so excited and just had to enter this but couldn't find DUMBOY on the Internet, the worldwide web or in the Arvig Telephone Directory. Fortunately, I found someone in Park Rapids who said he'd take my $250 and enter me into the contest. Thanks, Henry.

We just got two feet of snow in early December, so I started right away. I used my snowblower about every other day to keep the edges of the driveway neat. It was harder to keep the surface perfectly white and smooth. Henry found an electric Driveway Polisher for a mere $3000, paid in modest monthly payments after a $2000 down payment. The machine looked just like a floor polisher that I'd seen in a local hardware store, but Henry said it was specifically for winter driveways. It would plug up with snow and debris every ten minutes, but it was well worth the frequent cleanings in my quest for first prize.

I made ice sculptures along the driveway—a dog, a deer, a spruce tree, an elf and a cabbage. Sometimes I'd work into the wee, cold hours of the morning, and I probably spent six to eight hours per day on the project.

Well, the winter went by fast and March 15 finally arrived. On March 17 Henry notified me that I'd indeed won FIRST PRIZE. I pocketed the $15, and Henry will frame the beautiful certificate for only $25.

You can't believe the accolades from friends and everyone who'd heard about this. They varied from "Wow, Bob, that's quite the driveway you've got there," to "He's really flipped out this time, hasn't he?" My reputation has become the envy of all, and I'm the talk of the town.

Ah, I so love winter and am so appreciative of Henry and DUMBOY for allowing me to participate in this wonderful contest. I'll never forget it. Bob.

Chuck Kausalik-Boe

Poetry

Ballroom Slippers

She felt pensive as she gazed
around the apartment for rent.
Intuitively, she sensed a mist, like a fog.
She stumbled over the old shag carpet
as she entered the bedroom.
Opening the closet door,
she was confronted by a
lonely pair of ballroom slippers
tossed carelessly on the floor.
The sight of the ballroom slippers
brought a lump to her throat.
The color of the ballroom slippers
reminded her of the ocean
that haunted her dreams.

Wait

She breaks and breaks
The driftwood groans open
The instruments crack and rust
The roots in their secret places atrophy
Again and again.

So the small animals scatter from their life boat
So the saxophone wails without form
So the roots become earth

She
In her secret place,
Waits.

Stranger things have happened
Than what she is waiting for—
Birds have stayed north in the winter and
Mushrooms have composed subterranean suites that forests have no
                   choice but to
Follow

She knows that the manmade crumble—
Why she closes her eyes on planes
And hums to herself on bridges
The transience of buildings
Which long to sway like dancers
And governments, marriages, McDonalds, and computers
They all shine like the unstable

She knows that the women wait
And grow
Secretly
Like the river-swept log washed onto a bank
Covered with new moss and creatures
The wink of a seed

Cindy Fox

Creative Nonfiction

Clean & Repeat

The freshly laundered lace curtains I'd hung up three weeks ago are now stuffed over the curtain rods. The third and last weekend of deer hunting season and only one measly buck downed, the windows must expose maximum viewing range. Hunting clothes, reeking of spilled doe scent, are piled on my living room couch. Rifles lean against doorjambs, ready to assault unwary deer. Sorels circle the wood stove and weep brown water. Wet woolen socks suck the varnish from my wooden chair backs that now look like they've been smeared with toothpaste. I choke down a sob and wonder why I'd bothered with fall house cleaning.

Though I'd scrubbed the refrigerator upstairs during my cleaning frenzy, I'd forgotten to clean out the box freezer downstairs. Teetering on the basement steps while clutching a cardboard box of packaged ground venison, I pray I don't fall headfirst onto the clammy floor.

Our basement will never be one of those cozy family rooms where you want to hang out. Like a dungeon, the ceiling joists are flossed with cobwebs. The cement walls and floor are damp and cold. At the bottom of the stairs, a chill runs up my spine when I see the freezer lid that should be sealed like tight lips. Crunchy ice boils from the lid corner like a festering cold sore.

Thankfully, we don't throw anything away that may still have some life in it. Our mini freezer now looks darn good. Since the big boy needs defrosting, I transfer frozen goods from big boy into little boy. I have enough frozen vegetables that you'd think I was a Doomsday Prepper. Without an ounce of room to spare, I slam down the lid.

At the bottom of the big freezer I find several frost-bitten items: A bag of chicken nuggets with a 2009 expiry date, a baggie marked "Cindy's Broken heart—11/20/2008" that looks like a piece of termite-infested wood but now I recall it's the heart I'd plucked from the buck I'd shot that year. Lastly, an orange Popsicle that's exploded under extreme weight.

While I get my exercise running up and down the stairs and prying slabs of ice from the freezer walls and flinging them into a cooler to reduce my sopping-up time, Jim has shot another deer. Looking like a redneck, he drives up to the house with a deer head strapped to the front of the four-wheeler and wears ragged coveralls held together with duct tape.

"Jim, I swear I'll burn those damn things whenever I find the place where you hide them. You'd think you didn't have a penny to your name. Why don't you wear your new coveralls?"

"This old pair is good enough," he says. "Besides, I don't want to get the new ones dirty. You have enough cleaning to do."

That I do, as I watch him walk across the kitchen floor with a trail of mud following him out the door.

Deborah Rasmussen

Poetry

Plate Tectonics

The house isn't really empty
when children grow up and go

but space expands
like when continents drift apart

and you slip
into an unexpected gap

not sure how to settle

or whether parted shores
will meet again

or where
or when

Elizabeth Weir

Poetry

Improbable

Improbable that I should pass
at the very moment
a dragonfly alights on
the wing of a dragonfly sculpture,
a lone piece of art, planted
in a Minnesota prairie.

Improbable that I should be here,
in distant Minnesota, with you;
that you should have come, uninvited,
to a Polish party in South Africa,
that we should have met,
you from Ireland, me from England.

Improbable that I should happen to land
on the apex of your cardiologist heart
that long-ago night; that we are here,
contented, far from our origins
among summer prairies, sun-glanced
wings, unlikely sculptures.

Jennifer Hernandez

Honorable Mention Fiction

Blind Date at Penny's Diner

It was a set up. No way I would have gone there, if I had known what my parents had in mind. I traveled halfway across the country. And for what? To sit at a table with a medical student I had never met, eating greasy burgers because they were "safe." I was so tired of safe. Didn't they know that? Why couldn't they accept it?

The whole objective of my having taken the teaching job in El Paso was to get away. To get away from my stifling hometown. To get away from my family's expectations of who I should be and who I should be with. Yet here I sat, at a diner so stereotypically American that it belonged in a 1950s movie set—in Omaha, Nebraska, of all places—a town where I knew no one.

Ama had said that they missed me so much. Said that Baba needed to see his baby girl, and he couldn't wait until the end of the school year. Said they had frequent flyer miles saved up and hotel points, too. And I believed them.

So now here I sat in a booth upholstered with blue vinyl, a Formica table separating me from the man my parents were hoping to make their newest son-in-law. The man that would "save" their youngest daughter from her crazy ideas of saving the world one immigrant student at a time.

He was nice enough, overdressed for the diner in a white collared dress shirt and conservatively patterned necktie, clean-shaven, polite. Boring. Boring, boring, boring. Like every potential husband they had placed before me, starting when I was eighteen years old. ("Never too soon to start thinking about the future!" my mother had trilled.)

I nibbled my burger, picked at my fries, chewed the ice left in the bottom of my Coke glass, and nodded along to his stories of med school. Boring, boring, boring.

I'd see my parents again in the evening, and then hop a flight the next morning back to *la frontera*. Back to the messy, noisy, frustrating, exhilarating life that I was making for myself.

Back to Jorge, who was so very not what my parents had in mind, and so very *not* boring.

Shelley Getten

Poetry

Poet

She left the house
three hours ago—
she returned with poems
and twigs in her hair.

Mary Lou Brandvik

Poetry

Gert

Gert lived by the railroad tracks.

One December evening she placed
      her glasses on the kitchen table
      and stood on a chair to lift
      two Christmas-wrapped boxes
      to the top shelf of her
      closet.

      She shrugged on her winter coat,
      pulled on her gloves and wrapped
      a scarf around her neck,
      remembering to turn off the lights
      as she closed the front door
      and turned to the railroad tracks.

"I could see her on the tracks and
blew the horn over and over and over,"
the engineer said, "but she never turned
and just kept walking."

Nicole Borg

Honorable Mention Poetry

After Office Hours

The poem
rubs against my pant leg, purring,
winds around my writing desk,
saunters on silent paws
to the hall, so only the tip
of its twitching, teasing tail
is visible, beckoning.
I am helpless not to follow.
I see it slip through the closing
door and into moonlight.
I step into a gray night, searching,
everything shades of black and white
like a '50s detective show.
The poem rounds a parked car,
its steps low and sleek.
I navigate alleyways,
lonely dumpsters, crumbling
brick facades all closed
for the night. Hardly clue
enough to keep me in
the chase. I adjust my fedora,
reach into my trench coat
for my pen, notebook.
My lit cigarette bobs
in the dark. This game
of cat and mouse could make
a merry fool of me.
But who is the mouse?

Gallia

I pushed off the side of the pool into a streamline, the only person swimming in sunny, sixty-degree Las Vegas. While others lounged in skimpy bikinis, I donned my red-and-black marbled one-piece swimsuit, red silicone cap, and mirrored goggles. The pool was long and narrow, each end like the bulb of a thermometer. Two bridges spanned over the center, about twenty yards apart. Before the second bridge, an orange buoy lay across the pool. I swam under it. At the end of the pool, a teenaged lifeguard leaned over.

"This side of the pool is closed." He pointed to the buoy.

A porous boundary, I thought.

He added, "It's blocked off for maintenance."

There were no signs of maintenance, but I said, "Okay. Thank you," and swam back. At the end, I noticed a young girl with thick, wavy, brown hair wearing a blue bikini, jumping in the pool alone. I swam to the end, turned, and headed back toward the buoy, where the lifeguard now stood sentry. I anchored my right arm, tucked in my chin, and executed a perfect flip turn sans wall before heading back. What proprioceptive abilities, he surely thought.

When I reached the end, I saw the girl trying to flip herself and giggling at the cattywampus results. Back toward the buoy, when I turned my head to breathe, I caught sight of small feet keeping up with me on the pool deck all the way to the lifeguard. I wondered if he'd told her to stop running on deck.

After swimming a mile, I moved to the hot tub. I put on my bifocal sunglasses, sunhat, and erected my book wall. Mere minutes elapsed before my little shadow slipped in beside me. I looked at the girl's full, friendly, expectant face. I considered for a second, closed my book, and took off my glasses.

"My name is Gallia. I am from Armenia," she enunciated carefully, her malachite-green eyes sparkling.

"My name is Jenny. I'm from Minnesota," I answered. She lit up like a kid who'd caught her first fish.

I asked how old she was. She used her fingers to show and said at the same time, "one" and "zero."

"Ten years old?" I asked.

"Yes!" She bounced as she nodded.

She said she had a brother in Russia who was "one" and "nine."

"Nineteen?"

"Yes!"

A lady with a brown bun and olive skin peeked around the bushes calling, "Gallia." I waved and smiled to show that I was harmless.

Gallia told me that she spoke Armenian, Russian, and some English. I told her she was a very smart girl to speak so many languages, and she glowed with pride. She told me a bit of her life. Each word seemed a well-chosen, hard-purchased gift.

"The talking stick is a Native American tradition used to facilitate an orderly discussion. The stick is made of wood, decorated with feathers or fur, beads or paint, or a combination of all. Usually speakers are arranged in a talking circle and the stick is passed from hand to hand as the discussion progresses. It encourages all to speak and allows each person to speak without interruption. The talking stick brings all natural elements together to guide and direct the talking circle." —Anne Dunn

This year, we received nearly 300 submissions from 134 writers. From these, the Editorial Board selected 96 poems, 22 creative nonfiction stories, and 21 fiction stories from 92 writers for inclusion in this volume.

Please submit again!

www.thetalkingstick.com
www.jackpinewriters.com

Without the following contributors in 2019, this
Talking Stick would not have been possible.
Thank you to everyone!

Benefactors
Harlan and Marlene Stoehr
Marilyn Wolff
Sharon Harris
Mike Lein

Special Friends
Niomi Rohn Phillips
Eric Chandler
Cathy Wood
Paula Hari
Luke Anderson
Sharon Chmielarz
Paisley Kauffmann
Sue Bruns
Steven Vogel
Margaret Marty

Good Friends
Susan McMillan
Peter Stein
Elizabeth Weir
Lane Rosenthal
Kristin Laurel
Polly Scotland
Dan McKay

Friends
Bernadette Handl Thomasy
John Harrigan

Dorothy Anderson
Lina Belar
James Bettendorf
Micki Blenkush
Nicole Borg
Kim M. Bowen
Mary Lou Brandvik
Janice Larson Braun
Ed Brekke-Kramer
H. A. Brown
Sue Bruns
Mary A. Conrad
Frances Ann Crowley
Norita Dittberner-Jax
Charmaine Pappas Donovan
Neil Dyer
Larry Ellingson
Christine Madline Ellsworth
Jeanne Emrich
Jeanne Everhart
Jennifer Fackler
Marsha Foss
Cindy Fox
Kathryn Ganfield
Shelley Getten
Katie Gilbertson
Matt Gregersen
Ilse Griffin
Marilyn Groenke
Christine J. Grossman
Marlys Guimaraes
Tara Flaherty Guy
Michael Hager
Laura L. Hansen
Sharon Harris
Audrey Kletscher Helbling
Jennifer Hernandez
Susu Jeffrey
Jennifer Jesseph
Mary Jones
Meridel Kahl
Paisley Kauffmann
Chuck Kausalik-Boe
Patricia Kemmerick
Kathryn Knudson
Sonja Kosler

Laura Krueger-Kochmann
Viola LaBounty
Kristin Laurel
David LeCount
Mike Lein
Dawn Loeffler
Linda Maki
Cheyenne Marco
Christine Marcotte
Julie Martin
Adam McFarlane
Susan McMillan
Christopher Mueller
Marsh Muirhead
Ryan M. Neely
Julia Silverberg Nemeth
Vincent O'Connor
Yvonne Pearson
Kathleen J. Pettit
Niomi Rohn Phillips
Adrian S. Potter
Deborah Rasmussen
Avesa Rockwell
Kit Rohrbach
Lane Rosenthal
Mary Schmidt
Ruth M. Schmidt-Baeumler
Richard Fenton Sederstrom
Victoria Lynn Smith
LeRoy N. Sorenson
Maurice Spangler
Doris Stengel
Anne Stewart
Marlene Mattila Stoehr
J. M. S. Swanson
Bernadette Hondl Thomasy
Peggy Trojan
Lucy Tyrrell
Joel Van Valin
Steven R. Vogel
Susan Niemela Vollmer
Laura Weinberg
Elizabeth Weir
Ben Westlie
Pam Whitfield
Cheryl Weibye Wilke